COLOR FOR ARCHITECTURE

COLOR FOR ARCHITECTURE

Tom Porter
and
Byron Mikellides

VNR **VAN NOSTRAND REINHOLD COMPANY**
NEW YORK   CINCINNATI   TORONTO   LONDON   MELBOURNE

This book was first published in the United Kingdom by
Studio Vista, a division of Cassell & Collier Macmillan
Publishers Limited.

Copyright © 1976 by Tom Porter and Byron Mikellides
Library of Congress Catalog Card Number 76-17745
ISBN 0 442 26619 7

Printed by Sackville Smeets Billericay
Published in 1976 by Van Nostrand Reinhold Company
A division of Litton Educational Publishing, Inc.
450 West 33rd Street, New York, NY 10001

3   5   7   9   11   13   15   16   14   12   10   8   6   4   2

Library of Congress Cataloging in Publication Data
Main entry under title:

Color for architecture.

  Bibliography: p.
  Includes index.
  1. Color in architecture. I. Porter, Tom.
II. Mikellides, Byron.
NA2795.C64   1976   729   76-17745
ISBN 0-442-26619-7

Contents

ACKNOWLEDGEMENTS
Grateful thanks are due to: Henry Bumstead, Universal City Studios, California;
Gene Davis, Washington; Doris Freedman, President, City Walls Inc. New York;
Sue Goodman, Oxford; F. J. Heath, The Tintometer Ltd., England; The Leverhulme
Trust, England; Oxford Polytechnic, England; Andréa Peskine, Ed Architects, Paris;
Gio Ponti, Milan; Charles D. Wheelwright, Johnson Spacecraft Centre, Houston;
John Willcocks, Senior Research Fellow, University of Leicester; Beverly T. Volk,
Executive Secretary, Philadelphia Art Commission.

The article by Oscar Newman, 'The Use of Colour and Texture at Clason Point', is
copyright © Oscar Newman, 1975 (all rights reserved).

Above all the authors would like to express their gratitude to the contributors who
have graciously prepared material and statements for inclusion in this book.

Preface by Sir Hugh Casson

'Science is what you know', wrote Lethaby fifty years ago. 'Art is what you do.' Unwittingly, perhaps, he made the two activities sound separate and opposed. Too often they are. Although, as we all know, scientists employ in their researches the intuitive leap as often as artists apply the discipline of reason to their work, it is still true that the two cultures seem to speak in different voices and seldom to each other. (There is no substitute, says one, for the innocent certainty of the artist. There is no certainty, says the other, only the slow assembly of data tested and observed.) Nowhere perhaps is this mutual mistrust more true than in the study and use of colour in our environment. This is where man needs — indeed craves — colour, and where, despite the lessons of history, he is deprived of it to an extent that the authors of this important and timely book regard as almost 'dangerous'. Scientists and artists make of colour a professional mystery. Architects — perhaps because they draw (and therefore think) in black and white — are either frightened of it or ignore it. The drab results are around for all of us to see.

At a time when our built environment has never been so difficult to know, to understand, to identify with (or above all, contribute to), the absence or misuse of colour as a vital and positively corrective force seems both inexplicable and tragic. It's not, of course, an easy problem. Man's response to colour — as the following pages will show — can be to the expert tiresomely variable. They are complicated, not always predictable, deeply affected by climate and cultural background, by the incidence of natural or artificial light — even by the state of his digestion. Yet although the reasons why one colour may appear at one time to be more 'pleasing' than another still elude description, there is a growing body of knowledge, tested, measured and agreed, upon the psycho-physiological effects of colour and upon how these effects can most usefully and imaginatively be achieved.

We know, in fact, that colour can be made to work for its living — to make objects look heavier (or lighter), space to seem warmer (or cooler), planes to advance or recede, even sounds to seem louder or softer. We know that colour can be used decoratively, symbolically, or therapeutically. It can be used to signal or to delineate, to stimulate or to depress, to give a sense of place and thus a sense of identity.

8

We know, too, that — luckily — no formula exists. Science can test, codify and inform. It cannot choose. Here the contribution of the artist — particularly during the last decade, which has seen him escape from the easel and the frame into wider three-dimensional fields — is crucial. The partnership of knowing and doing is indivisible. All the more welcome, therefore, is this unique and authoritative book, in which a number of distinguished experts in different fields — scientists and scholars, artists, psychologists and architects — have been encouraged to have their individually knowledgeable say, on everything from the behaviour of rhesus monkeys to the interior design of spacecraft. Particularly to be welcomed is the belief by which all contributors are inspired — that there is still no truer colour-responsive instrument to be found than man in all his variety, and that the best way to study colour is to use it.

Introduction

This book has been produced out of an awareness that colour, as a basic and vital force, is lacking from the built environment and that our knowledge of it is isolated and limited. Research studies carried out into the meaning and effects of colour have been spasmodic, and findings, if potentially useful to the designer, are often communicated in a language he finds difficult to understand.

Much work has to be done before we can fully understand the complexities and effects of colour, and it will take several decades before investigations provide answers to the many questions which will ultimately enable the environmental designer to use colour with some confidence. Meanwhile, in many other fields of design colour occupies a natural and intuitive part of the design process. In our present concept of the built environment, however, this element appears to have been ignored or avoided to a degree which the authors consider potentially dangerous to the future visual well-being of society.

If we are to avoid the possibility of future grey, monochromatic towns and cities, we must reorientate our concept of space-form relationships towards a deeper awareness of coloured space and coloured form. We must accept colour, not as a separate element, but as one totally integrated into the visual experience.

As our towns and cities grow in size and number, it seems that we are in danger of not only losing the natural landscape but also the wealth of colour we seem reluctant or ill-equipped to replace. The main aim, therefore, of this book is to strengthen links between the expertise of the artist and the architect and encourage a dialogue between the researcher and the environmental designer in the hope that we might foster a more fearless or experimental application of colour thinking to built space. In so doing we have avoided documenting the philosophies of those institutions and authorities whose restrictive legislation or so-called colour co-ordination program-mes have limited the use of architectural colour and played a full part in contributing to the present lack of colour in the urban landscape.

In order to present a comprehensive picture of the 'state of the art' we have invited written contributions from leading authorities from the world of creative design (fine art, graphic design and architecture) and from eminent researchers who work in experimental and architectural psychology, science and biology. All have been selected because of their contributions towards a more colourful and exciting environment or their dedicated study of this phenomenon in relation to the human experience.

The distinguished names of VICTOR VASARELY of France and VICTOR PASMORE of Britain need no introduction. Both have established major reputations in the world of fine art which are founded on their respective and distinctive visual languages. However, both painters have also become involved in the condition of the urban environment; the former founded the Vasarely Didactic Museum at Gordes which acts as a source of information and ideas concerning all aspects of the fight against the visual disturbances of the modern city, while Pasmore's name has, since 1954, been linked with the physical growth of Peterlee new town in County Durham where he directs the spatial and environmental aesthetic of the housing and road layout.

FABER BIRREN is often cited as the world's leading authority on colour. He is a consultant in the practical and functional aspects of colour and light as distinguished from the aesthetic. He has applied findings from research in psychology, medicine and ophthalmology in the design of schools, hospitals, offices and factories. Apart from writing many books and papers on the subject, he has produced manuals of colour practice for the U.S. Army and Navy and for the British Ministry of Health.

The eminent American architect JOSEPH ESHERICK is also Professor of Architecture within the questioning atmosphere of the Berkeley campus. His San Francisco practice (Esherick, Homsey, Dodge & Davis) has received many citations in the form of awards, prizes and international exhibitions which testify to his position as one of America's leading designers. Colour plays a vital role in his design thinking and this is reflected in many of his Californian buildings. A recent project was the design of seven stations for the San Francisco Bay Area Rapid Transit (BART) — the first mass transit network to be implemented in the USA for sixty years.

Other architects who have contributed material include RICHARD ROGERS of Piano and Rogers (London, Paris and Genoa), FOSTER ASSOCIATES (London), ANNA and RICARDO BOFILL (Taller de Arquitectura, Barcelona) and JEAN DEROCHE — a leading member of AUA (Atelier d'Urbanisme et d'Architecture), Paris. All have used rich colour as an integral part of their design processes and later discuss their respective philosophies.

From the number of practising architects who have contributed material, OSCAR NEWMAN (Director, The Centre for Residential Security Design Inc., New York) and PETER SMITH (Director of the Design and Psychology Research Unit, University of Sheffield) are designers and researchers who are particularly concerned with environmental psychology. Both are authors of books which explore basic human drives in relation to the modern environment. In *The Dynamics of Urbanism* Smith relates urbanism, architecture and psychology. Although not a psychologist he has been deeply interested in the field for many years and his approach offers a glimpse of how a new kind of dialogue between architects and psychologists may inform the environmental design process. Oscar Newman's investigations into the relationships between inhuman urban behaviour and architectural design are well documented in his book *Defensible Space*. As part of a programme to upgrade Clason Point, a public housing development in the Bronx, New York City, he introduced strong colours to the façades and we invited him to discuss his philosophy, approach and observed responses to the colour modifications.

The movement towards the concept of the 'polychrome city' seems to have begun in France where JEAN-PHILIPPE LENCLOS, the leading *coloriste,* works in close collaboration with architects in the creation of exciting and colourful urban spaces. Lenclos explains his objective process of analysis which attempts to codify the language of existing environmental colour and acts as a reference source for his vibrant colour prescriptions for modern buildings and industrial machinery.

The work of DEBORAH SUSSMAN together with PAUL PREJZA (Deborah Sussman & Co.,

Santa Monica, California) has included nearly everything short of designing a building. Their extremely colourful attitude and approach to a broad range of design problems comes from two related sources: Miss Sussman's work at the Eames office and her travels through Mexico, India, North Africa and Europe. Her exuberant and intuitive use of colour in graphics and interior design stems from detailed observations and responses to the wealth of visual phenomena encountered in the villages and marketplaces of the world.

As part of his Environmental Light and Colour course at the Massachusetts Institute of Technology, PROFESSOR ROBERT PREUSSER supervises architectural experiments with coloured light articulated in interior and exterior space. Professor Preusser, whose long association with Gyorgy Kepes is well known, believes that the built environment would benefit from a wider application of more strongly coloured illumination and he questions the myth which has, hitherto, restricted its widespread use.

DR NICHOLAS HUMPHREY is Assistant Director of Research at the Sub-Department of Animal Behaviour, University of Cambridge. As a zoologist he is concerned by any suggestion that man is unique and believes that an aesthetic sense is widespread in nature being vital to animals in their struggle to survive. Dr Humphrey describes his exciting colour preference experiments with rhesus monkeys and his findings, set against the background of his evolutionary approach, might hold some significance for the designer.

As psychologist and art historian respectively, DR S. FRIEDMAN and SUSAN THOMPSON combine in their concern for the basic need for people to understand and participate in their surroundings. As a lecturer (Montclair State College, New Jersey) and co-author of *Environments: Notes and Selections on Objects, Spaces, and Behaviour,* Dr Friedman's consultancy or research is aimed at the more specific issues and relationships between the organism and its physical environment.

Colour has become increasingly important in the conquest of outer space. The research programme behind the design of spacecraft draws from existing colour psychology findings and investigations by various NATIONAL AERONAUTICS AND SPACE ADMINISTRATION research agencies using mock-ups and simulators. The NASA paper, which outlines a proposed application of colour to extraterrestrial interior design, is presented with the kind assistance of Charles D. Wheelwright (Johnson Spacecraft Centre, Houston).

The eminent scientist ANDERS HARD (Director, Swedish Colour Centre Foundation, Stockholm) has kindly accepted our invitation to present and explain his new version of the NCS (Natural Colour System) which, being formulated on our perception of colour, provides a breakthrough for research into the colour experience.

PROFESSOR CARL-AXEL ACKING and DR RIKARD KÜLLER, both from the Department of Theoretical and Applied Aesthetics, University of Lund, Sweden, have, for the past eight years, looked extensively into factors in the perception of the human environment. Using experimental methods such as models, films, simulated and actual full-scale room spaces they have undertaken several investigations into the perception of interiors with particular reference to colour.

Finally, DR LARS SIVIK (University of Göteborg) is one of the leading researchers to pioneer a more systematic analysis of the meaning of colours. His research activities have brought him into close contact with the Swedish Colour Centre and the experimental programme of Anders Hård. Apart from his methodological contribution, one of the most interesting aspects of his work has been a development from studies with colour samples to investigations of colour in architecture which he has followed by validation studies with existing coloured buildings in various parts of Sweden.

12

1 The Effects and Meaning of Colour (a short review)

Colour is part of a total sensory experience of our environment and contributes immeasurable beauty to the visual world. As an integral part of our perceptual system it helps us to identify and define objects in space and acts as a signalling device which is evidence of certain conditions, conveying information about our surroundings. It also indicates time inasmuch as colours change with time, altering during the day cycle and from one season to another.

As part of nature's 'survival kit' animals and plants are coloured for the functions of camouflage, attraction, protection and warning. Human animals are also widely coloured with races of pink, brown, black, red and yellow. Skin, hair and eye pigmentations vary from person to person and from race to race. We tend to select our clothing to complement or match our individual coloration. We also colour the insides of our living spaces. This seems to fulfil a basic need as we usually associate colour with happiness and lack of colour with boredom and sadness.

Colours are commonly divided into two temperature groups, those found at the 'warm' end of the spectrum and those at the 'cool' end. The warm colours, yellow through orange to red, are seen as aggressive or advancing. The cool colours, green through blue to violet, are generally considered as receding or passive, and are less clearly focused by the eye than the warm colours. This spatial effect has been noted by generations of painters who have understood that different areas of coloured paint can appear to occupy different positions in space — red appearing much closer to the observer than blue. A researcher (A. Ketcham) has claimed that the receding nature of blue is demonstrated by the apparent width of a parking space between two blue cars. The gap between them seems wider than it really is, and as a result, he suggests, blue cars suffer from more dented wings than those of other colours. In other experiments, the same researcher discovered that a noise sounded louder to a listener in a white room than the same noise heard in a violet room, and that a dark blue packing crate seemed to feel heavier than an identical crate coloured yellow.

Not only are certain colours associated with spatial reduction, expansion, weight and temperature but it is also claimed that their use in room spaces may induce occupants to feel warmer, to the extent of compensating for inadequate heating. In fact, laboratory experiments have shown that the colour red decidedly stimulates the nervous system — blood pressure rises, respiration rate and heart beat both speed up. By contrast, it has been found that blue has the opposite effect. In a blue room a person's blood pressure falls slightly, and the rates of heart beat and breathing slow down. A Norwegian study demonstrated that people would set a thermostat four degrees higher in a blue room than they would in a red one, as if to attempt a thermal compensation for the coolness that was visually induced.

In another study an American psychologist conducted an experiment where two identical twenty-minute lectures were presented to two separate audiences, one seated in a blue lecture theatre and the other in a red one. The 'blue' group felt rather bored and were under the impression that the lecture had lasted longer than the actual time, whereas the 'red' group found the lecture interesting and felt that the time had passed quickly. Similarly, the introduction of a deep red in the repainting of some factory toilets apparently, according to a report, much reduced the time spent in them by workmen.

Michelangelo Antonioni, the Italian film director, made an interesting observation during the making of his first colour film, *The Red Desert*. While shooting industrial scenes on location in a factory, he painted the canteen red in order to invoke a mood required as background to the dialogue. Two weeks later he observed that the factory workers had become aggressive and had begun to fight amongst themselves. When the filming was completed the canteen was repainted in a pale green in order to restore peace and so that, as Antonioni commented, 'The workers' eyes could have a rest'. Green has traditionally been thought of as a calming and restful colour and on this basis it was employed by the last governor of Alcatraz when redecorating the main cell-block and solitary confinement areas. Warmer, lighter colours were introduced into the corridors and, in an attempt to pacify his involuntary 'guests', all cells were painted green up to head height. In yet more unpleasant contexts, lime green particularly has been associated with nausea. It has been used in the colouring of gas chambers such as those at San Quentin.

Colour has been used therapeutically in dealing with emotionally and mentally ill patients in the belief that manic and aggressive patients need cool colours to calm them down, while depressive and suicidal patients cheer up to warm and exciting colours. However, the world of colour is full of contradictions and some recent research evidence suggests that the opposite may be more accurate, that excitable people need stimulating and active colours to help redirect their tensions while cool and calm colours may help the quiet and introverted. Colour research with brain-damaged patients found that warm and cool colours, particularly red and green light, exert quite different influences. Under red, speed of body movements increased together with the loss of equilibrium and perceptual distortion of size and judgement. It was also found that green light tended to minimize these abnormal conditions.

Green pigment was used in a pharmaceutical factory, but on this occasion to adjust a visual side-effect. Production-line workers checking purple pills complained of migraine and of seeing green spots in front of their eyes. This problem was solved by surrounding the employees with green-coloured screens against which the 'spots' did not show. The company management had realized that green is the negative after-image of purple-red, and that the green spots were merely after-images of the pills.

Clinicians and art-therapists have observed that suicidally inclined patients tend to use yellow pigment generously in their paintings — as, indeed, did Vincent Van Gogh. His last painting before committing suicide was the mainly yellow *Wheatfield with Crows*. There is also a widely held belief that the colour yellow stimulates the intellect and on this basis it has been prescribed as a suitable colour for libraries and classrooms. In another situation, the Institute of Contemporary Arts in London discovered to their cost that the stimulant effect of yellow is so intense that it can incite children to vandalism. During an exhibition of toys, displayed in various coloured rooms, all those in the yellow room were damaged or broken!

Faber Birren, the American colour consultant, has described experiments in which even blindfolded people have shown response to varying coloured stimuli. Colour-blind animals have also been physically affected by coloured light, especially in relation to their sexual behaviour, and according to experiments conducted by John Ott coloured light has a profound effect in determining the sex of rats, mink and fish. Breeding under blue illumination they apparently produce more females, and under red light more males. If these findings are correct, the old phrase 'blue for a boy and pink for a girl' is wildly out in the lower animal kingdom.

Most colours do not have easily measurable effects and a further complication is the fact that coloured illumination behaves in an entirely different way from surface pigment. Nevertheless, colour can create psychological reactions which, in turn, depend upon a number of interrelating factors — social class, age, personal taste, historical symbolism and cultural background.

Apart from adding a further dimension to shape and form, colour also acts as a kind of language. However, colour meanings vary from individual to individual and are dependent upon culture, and time. It seems probable that our attitudes to various hues emanate, to a great degree, from early learning processes and are, therefore, established on a cultural basis. We can also speculate that emotional responses to colour are closely linked with our ability to register colour directly on the brain but, on the other hand, we do know that there is some agreement amongst people in their attitudes to certain colours.

Red, for instance, is universally regarded as a warm and arousing colour and is symbolically used to represent aggression and revolution. The obvious link between red and the colour of blood is very strong, the word for 'red' can be traced back to the same origins as the word for 'blood' in many languages. In Western countries white represents purity, while in many eastern countries purity is represented by yellow, hence the saffron robes of the Buddhist monks. Yellow (and pink) in some oriental cultures has the same meaning as blue in the West, as in blue films and blue jokes. Similarly, in most Northern countries black or purple are the colours of grief and mourning but in some tropical areas white is worn.

The addition of colour to real objects produces strong feelings among many people and some colours are seen as 'wrong'. The unnatural quality of blue for food is one of the best-known examples. At the end of his journey through space and time David Bowman, the astronaut in *2001: A Space Odyssey,* arrives in a perfect replica of a hotel suite. Everything in this galactic apartment is fashioned to simulate an earthlike setting, all except the food he finds in the refrigerator, which is blue. In Arthur C. Clarke's novel, Bowman overcomes a deep-seated feeling that the blue substance may be poisonous, and on eating discovers the taste to be rather pleasant. Although most colour preference investigations suggest that blue is the colour most universally liked, we have a strong aversion to blue food. It was the authors' experience that a group of young children taking part in a test with dyed vegetables became decidedly ill after eating harmless blue-coloured potatoes. However, the same children in another test happily ate some specially prepared blue sweets as part of a colour preference experiment, favouring the novelty of blue — where artificiality is accepted — over the other range of standard colours.

From time immemorial colours, in the form of materials, pigments, dyes and stains, have carried symbolic meanings in their application to everyday artefacts, clothing, bodies and buildings, generally in relation to survival and worship.

Dr Max Lüscher, a Swiss psychologist, suggests that the passive connotation of blue and the energetic and vital association with yellow stem from the two factors which dictated the life-style of primitive man. Daybreak, characterized by the yellow light of the sun, heralded an environment in which action and the hunt for food could take place. The dark blue night sky brought an end to his aggressive phase and enforced his withdrawal to the safety of his refuge. This early significance of the colour of night and day might account for some of our more deep-seated colour responses such as the association of blue with isolation and sadness and the symbolism of yellow for vitality and happiness. But it is more likely that black was associated with night as the colour is usually linked with hostile and ominous qualities. Yellow was actually worshipped by the ancient Egyptians as part of a colour-coded system which assigned yellow to the sun god, and black to evil. They believed that colours embodied mystical powers and their temples were often painted with blue ceilings to represent the heavens and green-coloured floors to symbolize the fertile meadows of the Nile. Extremes in skin complexion were highly prized and the cosmetic application of colour was widely practised in order to intensify flesh coloration; even the face of the Sphinx was painted red.

The walls of the ancient Chinese capital of Peking were painted in red and roofs within the city coloured yellow. Red and yellow symbolized positive-negative and were also associated with good and evil spirits. The yellow roofs acted as a form of camouflage which blended buildings into the surrounding landscape, thereby protecting inhabitants from any evil spirits who happened to pass overhead. Similarly, only yellow rice is eaten by Indonesians as part of a ceremonial meal prepared to celebrate the completion of a house building.

Remnants of this symbolic use of colour still survive, although stripped of original meanings, in some present-day religions, heraldry, folk art and primitive architecture. Notwithstanding its decline, modern man is still motivated by basic needs which include an urge for colour in his everyday life. This urge is often not realized by environmental designers and, as a result, receives little satisfaction from the built environment. Recent experiments (reported later) on the responses to external colour in architecture by Dr L. Sivik of Göteborg, Sweden, and observations made by Oscar Newman in the United States of reactions to his colour proposals for external façades, indicate that people will accept much more intense colours in their environment than architects might predict or a 'sophisticated taste' would allow.

Studies of the evolutionary scale in animal behaviour by zoologists, such as Darling and Ardrey, suggest that territoriality does not only zone the physiological needs of animals but also the psychological desires: the need for security, stimulation and identity. It is not surprising to find that human motivations and behaviour are usually compared to the animal studies as, it is thought, they are determined by those same needs. Investigations into 'sensory deprivation' help to ascertain the extent to which we are dependent upon stimulation from our environment and the tests, which study subjects in almost total sensory isolation, have produced findings which appear to be conclusive. Research work in this field has been carried out by Professor D. O. Hebb of McGill University, Canada and Professor J. Vernon of Princeton University in the United States. The latter has proposed a theory to account for 'sensory deprivation' in terms of our need for a changing stimulation. He states, 'The human cannot long endure a homogeneous situation no matter how good and desirable it is.' And 'In "sensory deprivation" there is no variation and any small stimulus, such as a faint light, becomes as enjoyable as a desirable experience.'

Neurologists have also suggested that the nervous system not only reacts to stimulation but to changes in stimulation; Dr Eric Miller has said that the brain needs constantly varying forms of stimulation in order to operate in relation to the environment. In support, J. Vernon modified the old saying when he wrote, 'Variety is not only the spice of life, it is the very stuff of it.'

Once our need for security is satisfied, we seek identity and stimulation. The desire for a distinct ego-identity and self-esteem can be seen in the way we use colour to personalize our clothes, personal possessions and the interiors of our homes. The search for stimulation in the external environment may have responded to those richer, more elaborate styles of architecture which have occurred from time to time, but it is expressed in what is now known as 'Pop Architecture'. This phenomenon, directly echoing public taste, is rich in symbolism, decoration and, especially, colour, as it is diametrically opposed to the hardness and uniform greyness of the forms produced by the modern architectural movement.

Responses to environmental stimuli are complex as they are interrelated and interdependent. We consider colour to be an important factor and that, as an element which can play a vital and integral role in urban design, it has the capacity of both increasing our overall level of response and the means of providing a changing stimulus.

We hope that, through a study of the various research findings and philosophies, we might establish a deeper awareness of the potential of environmental colour, which in turn might create a more colourful urban structure.

The Need for Colour and Light in Future Man-Made Spaces

Faber Birren

With little colour in our modern towns and cities we are ill-equipped to incorporate colour into the design processes of future environments. Our urban centres are becoming progressively artificial and soon they will be almost totally man-made. In this developing situation, designers will have to answer questions they have never faced before; questions concerning controlled environments, radiation, and the effects of artificial light and colour on man, animals and plants.

Faber Birren, the eminent colour consultant and world authority on the functional application of colour, explains why we should study the newer scientific research in order to equip ourselves for the future:

Colour in architecture today is too bland, too sweet, too much a luxury. A preponderance of white and grey walls is emotionally sterile and visually dangerous. As modern civilization grows more complex, the environmental designers will need a better understanding of the psychic make-up of people. Other factors than colour need study, but at least the specification of it can avoid a mere personal fancy on the part of the architect or interior designer who should profit from sound research.

The gradual movement of people out of the natural environments and into the man-made ones is a trend, it seems, that cannot be reversed. With urbanization, population explosions and the resultant pollution of nature, there simply isn't room enough to allow every man his garden and tree and at the same time maintain efficient channels of transportation and communication. Men of future generations will not only travel in space but possibly live there. They will live under the sea and within domed cities. Life will be extremely complicated — and artificial.

Light and colour are essential to all forms of life. Plant growth depends upon it. Lower and higher animals react to it. Length of day is responsible for bird migration and for the mating habits of mammals. Radiant energy, accepted through the eye or as it penetrates living tissue, stimulates glandular response, metabolism, hormone development, the entire autonomic system — respiration, heart action and appetite.

However, not all coloured light sources offer the same benefits. Since the invention of artificial illuminants, from oil and gas to electricity, the effort has been to enable man to see. There has been light for vision. Some of this artificial light has had fairly natural qualities: kerosene, paraffin candles, illuminating gas and the early carbon filament electric light bulbs. Some of it has been anything but natural: mercury and sodium vapour, neon and fluorescent. Yet for the purposes of seeing, whatever could be economically produced was acceptable.

Quite recently, however, the lighting industry has been aware of the need for biological lighting, for illumination that will help to sustain life itself. There is now clear evidence that incomplete or unbalanced light can have hostile effects. A mouse, or a man, would not thrive if exposed solely to mercury or sodium vapour light. Where artificial light does not have some equivalence to sunlight, trouble may be encountered. Biological lighting requires a balance of spectral energy, light that is close to sunlight and daylight in quality, if not in degree of intensity. Such light should include a limited amount of ultra-violet radiation. Therefore, we can look at biological lighting as a requisite for the human environments of the future.

A key dilemma of the artificial, man-made environment may be centred around what is known today as sensory deprivation or perceptual isolation. This introduces a psychological problem to the biological one: if man can be given the proper balance of light to keep his body functioning, he will also need sensory stimulation to keep his spirit and soul together. This involves colour and other sensory interests.

18

There should be a resourceful and dynamic use of colour in the environment itself — for proper mental and emotional balance. Colour in built space serves two highly important purposes. In the realm of vision it can remove glare from the field of view. If the colour is warm and cheerful, it can also direct attention outward and make a person alert to what is going on around him. If the colour is cool and a little muted, the environment will be less distracting and the person will be better able to concentrate on visual and mental tasks. In the realm of emotion, colour can introduce sensory stimulation, break up monotony, establish an interesting change of pace. It is not just that one colour is better than another, or that red is exciting, green tranquil and blue subduing. What has been learned from research is that variety is, of itself, psychologically beneficial.

As the advance of civilization pens man more and more away from nature he must command and utilize to the fullest all the factors that can help maintain his well-being and sanity. Light and colour are amongst those factors.

The Dialectics of Colour

Dr Peter Smith

Dissatisfaction with cities is growing, and the expression of this dissatisfaction is becoming more articulate. Dr P. F. Smith – Director of the Design and Psychology Unit, University of Sheffield – believes that architects are not entirely to blame but considers it important that they attempt to discover how the built milieu might be more fulfilling through a study of the psychological needs that urbanism can satisfy.

It is possible to detect two trends in contemporary psychology. One perhaps constitutes a reaction against the behaviourist belief that attitude and behaviour are solely conditioned by experience. Now it is becoming increasingly feasible to believe that information in some organized form can be transmitted genetically. The dynamic psychologists were drawn to this conclusion on clinical evidence. Noam Chomsky later concluded that there are certain collective 'deep structures' forming archetypal rules of language. Most recently, developmental psychologists have been demonstrating that even new-born infants have a degree of perceptual ability which can have no basis in experience.

The other trend in recent psychology concerns the anatomy and physiology of the brain, with a view to throwing new light on human attitudes and actions. This neurophysiological research falls into two clear patterns. On the one hand there is interest in the interaction between the higher brain, or neocortex, and the various organs within the mid-brain and brain stem regions, termed the limbic system.

What is becoming clear is that the limbic system plays a decisive role in perception. It is now believed that there are two systems of visual perception, one which includes conscious experience in the process, and another which excludes conscious, rational mentation, and directly involves the limbic system. Some fibres of the optic nerve link directly with the limbic system via the superior colliculus. Animal experiments in which the occipital cortex is removed have proved that the mid-brain has its own visual syntax and can achieve a primitive level of seeing.

The other sphere of interest in neuropsychology focuses on the neocortex itself, and is particularly concerned with the fact that it is divided into right and left cerebral hemispheres which have contrasting attitudes to information. The pioneer of bilateral psychology is Roger Sperry, a surgeon from the United States. He discovered that each half is capable of 'independent sensation, perception, learning and memory processes' (J. Sault, 'The Human Brain', *Doctor*, 23 November 1972). By means of experiments with patients in whom the connecting fibres between the hemispheres had been severed to relieve epilepsy, Sperry offered conclusive evidence that the left hemisphere is the centre of verbal and serial mathematical ability. It is the seat of logic and rational deduction. In contrast, the right side is efficient at processing abstract, non-verbal information, and handles spatial perception. It responds to texture, colour and tone, and is biased towards discovering patterns of coherence. Since it has a strong interest in the way things fit together to form a closed system, it may be said to be a decisive factor behind the aesthetic response. The fundamental difference is summed-up by Roger Lewin: 'Sequential information processing occurs in the left hemisphere and simultaneous processing in the right' ('The Brain's Other Half', *New Scientist*, 6 June 1974).

This difference is reflected in the anatomical structure of each hemisphere. The cell and nerve patterns of the left side are noticeably more refined and sophisticated than those of the right, facilitating high focal acuity. The wider scanning ability possessed by the right seems to be a direct consequence of its coarser structure.

From the point of view of colour perception, it is obviously the right hemisphere which is the relevant sub-system of the neocortex. This point, however, should be related to the fact that the primitive visual syntax of the limbic brain includes an ability to recognize certain colours strong in chroma and brightness. The primitive brain responds to anything that is exotic: bright colour or things which glitter. This may be a residual response, developed during an earlier phylogenetic stage when the higher functions of the neocortex had barely begun to develop.

MacLean believes that the limbic system contains information structures — 'ancestral lore and ancient memories' (medical paper, 1964, cited by A. Koestler in *The Ghost in the Machine,* Hutchinson, London). He also attributes to the limbic brain a capacity for symbolic responses, with particular reference to colour: 'though the visceral brain (limbic system) could never aspire to conceive of the colour red in terms of a three letter word or a specific wavelength of light, it could associate the colour symbolically with such diverse things as blood, fainting, fighting, flowers, etc.' (*op. cit.*). To this list should be added fire, a most important associate of 'redness'.

What is now emerging is that the brain exhibits three attitudes to colour information. The right cerebral hemisphere appears to have the monopoly of perceiving colours outside the limited range of the primary and exotic. It is responsive to the more subtle colours which are described as 'cerebral' or 'sophisticated'.

The limbic system has two attitudes to colour. First it is responsive to high chroma, brightness, shine and glitter for their exotic quality; their sheer impact potential. Secondly it ascribes symbolic meaning to certain high chroma colours: a symbolic programme with archetypal origins.

The limbic system contains the hypothalmus which is responsible, amongst other things, for the exteriorization of emotion. Because of the rich and intimate connections within the limbic system, any limbic-intensive response invariably contains an emotional element.

One of the characteristics of great art is that it generates a critical tension between elements evoking a cerebral response, and features generating emotion. It may do this through content or via the medium. Artists like Rembrandt, Turner and Rouault achieved this bi-polar tension through both medium and message. Piet Mondrian strikes this critical balance predominantly through colour stripped of cognitive meaning.

Architects in the contemporary mode have little predilection for the emotional in design since it is equated with vulgarity. So 'architectural' colours are those which are supremely cerebral. For limbic satisfaction it is necessary to go to market places, Piccadilly Circus or Las Vegas.

The aesthetic implications of all this are profound. The aesthetic experience is a special kind of dialectic reaction within the mind to external stimuli upon the mind which superimposes pattern and coherence. When that coherence embraces features drawing a response both from the neocortex and the limbic system, the result is 'high amplitude' aesthetics, or an experience with a strong emotional component.

More than ever, there is a need for environmental presentations which enable the neocortex and limbic system to experience creative synthesis. Redevelopment in cities invariably succeeds in eliminating features which satisfy the need for the exteriorization of emotion. Thus cities are consistent with the wider cultural ethos which attaches maximum value to cerebral matters, and in particular, those of the left hemisphere.

Colour in environment has a crucial role to play both in keeping alive the cerebral interactive rhythms by nourishing the needs of the right side, and by keeping active the dialectic routes between the centres of reason and emotion.

When the wavelength profiles of colours perceived on different levels of the brain orchestrate into synchronous rhythms, the result is a special kind of experience, which, in the old days, was called beauty. Now, we would be better calling it therapy.

21

2 Colour in the Architectural Environment

(1) The Primitive and Ancient Environment: The Modern Concept of Form

Throughout history it has been believed that colour affects the well-being and health of man. Its power was appreciated by the primitive caveman and it played an important role in his struggle to survive. He projected his perceptions of this struggle on to the walls of his cave in the form of painted images. His use of colour was not only applied to enhance form and shape but carried a potent, magical meaning which was more vital to his continued existence than the aesthetic value we place on it today. The range of colours used in the Lascaux cave in France is vast and seemingly more striking than the actual design. Apart from identifying figurative forms, colour was also used, apparently for its own sake, in abstract designs painted high on the walls of the cave.

Many such caves have been discovered but are obviously only a small fraction of the colourful underground spaces which once existed. Lascaux and the caves at Ariège and Altamira testify to an early craving for colour — the polychromatic cave dwelling being entirely acceptable to the mentality of primitive man. This first spontaneous involvement with colour was later directed towards external spaces by builders. As the use of colour moved out of the underground caves and into the sunlight, and as knowledge of pigments increased, architectural colour became richer.

It is thought that colour was used purely symbolically during the ancient civilizations as it is today in primitive cultures. Among the primitives there still exists no real difference between building and image-making so far as usefulness is concerned. Their shelters function simply to protect them from the elements and coloured images are made to protect them from the spiritual powers which are felt to be as real as the forces of nature. It is interesting to note that this use of colour occurs in almost all primitive and ancient cultures of the world, and that always the same type of strong, saturated hues are used: notably red, blue, yellow, green, black and white, together with the precious metals — silver and gold. It has been speculated, and research lends support (I. R. Kohn, 1967), that the psychological primaries of red, green, blue and yellow are related to the primary emotions. This might explain their overwhelming use as symbolic colours. However, the main factor which

22

confuses a comparison of symbolism between cultures is that colours can be used to signify so many different concepts, and that these concepts are dependent upon the structure of a given society. The uses of symbolic colour mainly functioned in areas such as religion, mythology and astrology, ceremonial occasions, for healing purposes, and to denote social status, races, the elements of science and points of the compass.

It is believed that the Mesopotamian civilization was dominated by the study of astrology and that colour, being assigned to the solar system, was also related to the vertical and horizontal forms of their architecture. An example of the ordered ranking of colour in their built environment is found in a description of the city, Ectabana, by Herodotus in the fifth century B.C. He described the city as a conurbation of great size fortified by concentric coloured walls, each designed so that successive walls were higher than the one below by the height of its battlements. There were seven such walls built on a hill which exaggerated the cuneiform appearance of the city. The inner wall contained the royal palace and treasury and its battlements were plated with gold. The battlements of successive walls were plated in silver, painted in orange, blue, crimson, black, and the outer wall, white.

In his book *Ur of the Chaldees,* C. L. Wooley describes the 'Mountain of God'. Dated at 2,300 B.C. it is one of the oldest buildings in history. This ziggurat was built in four stages: the lowest wall was black and represented the dark underworld and the upper wall was red representing the habitable earth. At the very top was a blue tiled shrine with a gilded metal roof, signifying the heavens and the sun. The colour of the city of Ectabana must have also been based on similar principles.

The dazzling quality of sunlight had a profound effect on architectural painting in ancient Egypt. The Egyptians' environmental colour sense was extremely lively and was expressed in even, decided and sometimes quite violent tones, but it could also be delicate and faint. They loved to juxtapose contrasting colours in a manner which reveals a deep feeling for the unique quality of each particular hue. This positive application of colour to their buildings and statuary accentuated architectural detail in a climate where plastic form, if softly modelled, would appear diffused. They also evolved a highly developed language of colour which was so precise that it became an important element in hieroglyphics — their representational picture writing.

The Egyptian use of symbolic colour, being related to their deity system, and that of Mesopotamia, was passed on via Asia Minor to Greece where it became adapted to fit a new form of religion. Although the culture of the ancient Greeks was more influential than any other on our present-day Western civilization, and much is known about their architecture and society, until recently little was known about their use of colour.

However, if Athens had suffered the fate of Pompeii and Herculaneum its emergence from the preserving action of the volcanic ashes would have changed our concept of the visual appearance of the ancient Greek capital. A walk along one of its streets would prove to be something of a colourful experience for most of the houses and temples would be found to be painted in symbolic, and sometimes cosmetic, colouring — some statues even wearing 'lipstick', false eyelashes and possibly precious stones simulating flashing eyes in their flesh-coloured stone heads. Only gold and silver would be seen to be unpainted within this predominantly white, blue, red and yellow environment.

The ancient Greeks almost entirely covered their architecture with colour washes in the belief that the natural coloration of wood, marble, ivory and bronze was no substitute for the artistic creation of the city as a total art form. Many scholars had thought that early Greek architecture used little applied colour. This is easy to understand as there was very little evidence of it due to the fact that the climate of Greece is much wetter than that of Egypt and the exposed pigments deteriorated quickly. C. W. Ceram's description of freshly unearthed remains perhaps best illustrates the Greeks' love of colour: 'The plastic works of the ancient Greeks were gaily coloured. Statuary was deeply dyed with garish pigments. The marble figure of a woman found on the Athenian Acropolis was tinctured red, green, blue and yellow. Quite often statues had red lips, glowing eyes made of precious stones and even artificial eyelashes.' Again with regard to statuary, an unknown author describes an excavated pediment: 'Flesh, reddish in tone; globe of eyes yellow, iris green, with a hole in the centre filled with black; black outlines to eyebrows and eyelids; hair and beard bright blue at the time of excavation, which disintegrated later into a greenish tone; circle of brown around the nipples.'

The Greek use of environmental colour was eagerly adopted by the Romans whose over-riding interest in coloured buildings was displayed by their use of materials: brightly coloured paints and marbles, gold, bronze and mosaics. However, being a more practical people, they restricted the application of colour to buildings and left sculpture unpainted. Excavations at Pompeii by Johann Wincklemann between 1762 and 1767 uncovered a range of bright and deep pigment which was much wider and, in some cases, much clearer than the Greek colours.

The immense influence of the Roman Empire extended over almost the whole of Western Europe and, later, medieval architectural forms were covered with colour. During this period colour was richly and enthusiastically applied to the internal and external faces of important buildings as applied pigment, gilding, and in the form of stained glass windows.

Traces of colour are still distinguishable on the façades of Notre Dame in Paris, and James Ward wrote of this: 'The colouring occurred principally on the mouldings, columns, sculptured ornaments and figurework. The outside colouring was much more vivid than the inside work. There were bright reds, crude greens, orange, yellow ochre, blacks and pure white, but rarely blues, outside, the brilliancy of light allowing a harshness of colouring that would not be tolerable under the diffused light of the interior,' and 'There is also evidence that the greater portion of similar edifices of the thirteenth, fourteenth and fifteenth centuries in France were decorated in colour.'

It was not only in France that the exteriors of Gothic buildings were decorated in this way; it also occurred in England, an example of which is quoted by Cecil Stewart in his book, *Gothic Architecture:* 'The great west front of Wells, with its one hundred and seventy-six full-length statues was brilliantly coloured. The niches were dark red, and the figures and drapery were painted a yellow ochre, with the eyes and hair picked out in black and the lips in red.'

Colour was obviously of great importance to the people of the Middle Ages, and perhaps the 'vulgar' and spontaneous way in which it was used is a direct reflection of the spirit of the people at that time. Possibly this may be responsible for the reaction against it and its subsequent removal by the ensuing Puritan movement.

We have documented these examples of polychromatic architecture to illustrate the early concept of a built environment which included rich colour as an essential component. In order to begin to understand the present lack of colour in the modern environment we must return to the Greek classical style of architecture which has served as a source of inspiration to architects through the ages. However, the subsequent interpretations have been based on a fundamental misconception. The Parthenon, for example, has generally been taken as the epitome of architectural perfection. Our image of this marble structure as a symbol of freedom and democracy has led to the erection of many imposing buildings in our modern cities which imitate its style and proportion in concrete and stone. The idea that the Parthenon would come to be a source of study in monochromatic excellence would have puzzled Ictinus and Callicrates because they had originally designed it to be completely painted, gilded and detailed in rich colours (figure 2). Our modern image of this temple is in direct contrast to its actual appearance in 447 B.C. but its function as a symbol of purity remains the same.

The basic reason for the difference between these contrasting concepts of the Parthenon and, indeed, for our lack of understanding of the visual qualities of other ancient cities was probably caused by the impermanence of the colours used at the time. Rich environmental colours were eroded by the ravages of time and historians and architects came to accept the exposure of the natural surfaces of building materials as the colouring of ancient buildings.

The exceptions to this natural process of deterioration and loss of colour are those caves, tombs and cities which became suspended in time by the accidents of natural forces and the preservation instinct of ingenious men. The prehistoric caves in France and Spain, Egyptian and Etruscan burial chambers, Pompeii and Herculaneum all act as time capsules which provide us with a direct visual link with the rich use of colour in the past. Their comparatively recent discovery came too late for the ancient love of architectural colour to have any real influence on our established misconception of the past.*

Each discovery came as a shock to our understanding, and when Alma-Tadema, in 1868, correctly depicted the Elgin marble frieze as coloured in his painting *Phidias and the Parthenon* he shocked the idealists and caused something of a minor scandal. In his disbelief Auguste Rodin, the sculptor, is reported to have struck his heart crying, 'I feel here that these were never coloured'.

The extent of our misconception is graphically illustrated by historical sets for epic Hollywood films such as *Helen of Troy, Spartacus, Ben Hur*, etc. Charlton Heston and Kirk Douglas acted out their historic roles against cardboard reconstructions of a white, marbled ancient Greece and imperial Rome. This celluloid misrepresentation complies with and reinforces our concept of unpainted past environments. It is hardly surprising then that our more recent attitudes and design philosophies are thoroughly conditioned against the conscious use of colour in our external city environment.

*The cave at Altamira was discovered in 1863 and in 1879 the presence of the coloured paintings was first detected. Tutankamun's tomb was discovered and opened in November, 1922.

(2) The Separate Paths of Architecture and Art:
The Modern Concept of Space

Victor Vasarely, the leading French Op Art painter, uses colour in ingenious geometric patterns to generate ambiguous and reversible illusions. Recently he has become concerned about the isolation of the artist and his work and has shown much interest in the design of the environment. Eager himself to break free from the limitation of the picture frame and to redirect his colour–form expertise to the urban situation, he attempts to explain the division between the creative activities of the artist and the architect.

According to his theory this split dates back to the Renaissance, and results from two major influences: firstly, the increased separation and specialization of roles within art and science; secondly, the birth of the notion of a 'work of art', which was encouraged by an interest in the surviving relics of the ancient Roman culture.

During the Middle Ages, painters and sculptors were craftsmen who worked within building construction teams. However, the advent of humanism and quest for knowledge in the *Quattrocento* triggered off a creative outburst which led to the gradual separation of architecture and art into distinct avenues of study. Each branch of intellectual activity became isolated one from another and building, sculpture and painting existed on their own terms. Not only was the artist's identity separated in this way but his work became divorced from its hitherto architectural context and for the first time artists formed themselves into groups or schools.

Initially, carved objects and painted images were designed for specific buildings but as the idea of an 'art for art's sake' grew, built spaces were tailored to house them.

A further cause for the divorce between art and architecture appears to stem from the beginnings of archaeology. This new-found interest in the past began earlier in the 1440s when Flavio Biondi, who has been called the father of archaeology, systematically catalogued the surviving remains of imperial Rome. Up until that time the architectural glories of the ancient Roman culture had been left to rot. The Forum, for example, was partially buried and used both as a grazing field for cattle and as a convenient city quarry for building materials.

The subsequent excavations in the city transformed Rome into a vast museum and a fashion was started for the collecting of relics as 'art objects'. Both Filippo Brunelleschi and Donato Donatello compiled private collections of found objects which were to have a profound influence on the direction of their work and, indeed, on the subsequent development of sculpture and architecture as separate art forms.

Wealthy Italian patrons not only collected the archaeological finds but also commissioned paintings and sculpture by contempory artists. This, for the first time, isolated the artist's products as entities or 'works of art' to be viewed out of context from their original architectural setting.

The Renaissance had caused creative men to reject the almost redundant idea of symbolic colour as part of an environmental language and turn, instead, towards an individual translation of the colours of the real world. Closer observations were made of the changing colours of nature. Leonardo da Vinci meticulously began to examine the spatial behaviour of colour, recording in words and paint the effect of light and weather on the colour of objects in space.

Colour had, therefore, become more naturalistically and creatively employed in the painter's investigation of space, whilst the sculptor involved himself with an examination of the interaction and contrast between solid form and the empty space surrounding it.

Our legacy from the Renaissance is the twentieth-century notion of form and volume which has developed from an understanding of space as defined by the visual elements — form, shape, line, texture and colour. Most present-day design courses

26

are founded on this principle, which was expounded at the Bauhaus by teachers including Johannes Itten, Paul Klee and Wassily Kandinsky. Their educational philosophy, examining as it does the spatial experience and design co-ordination in component parts, has contributed a great deal to the designer's understanding. He is much more aware of the diversity and potential of formal arrangements. However, this fragmentation of approach to spatial analysis and the design process appears to have isolated colour as a separate and neglected element. A contributory factor to this neglect is the nature of the environmental designer's visual language which, from the evidence available, seems to have changed little since the Renaissance.

The perfection of perspective by Brunelleschi in the early fifteenth century had a significant effect on the visualization and organization of three-dimensional elements. It enabled the architect to master the linear representation of spatial dimensions and explore his concepts more accurately before the construction stage. Perspective, plans, elevations and projection drawings have since become the traditional methods used in communicating architectural ideas. Graphics are usually drawn or 'rendered' in black and white and even small-scale models, which are also part of this communication process, are constructed with a greater concern for achromatic plastic qualities than the manipulation of coloured form in space.

This, together with the later influence of black and white photography, appears to have isolated form as a colourless substance. Architecture and sculpture, until very recently, have been preoccupied with the manipulation of form using a design approach which is closely connected with the modern concept of 'pure' or colourless space. It seems strange that a designer of real spaces for habitation by real people should externalize his spatial concepts as illusions of three-dimensional reality on paper and employ a philosophy which excludes, to a great degree, any colour consideration.

As a result, the complexity of the behaviour of spatial colour has never been fully understood or investigated in the environmental context. Colour expertise is now in the hands of the painter who carries out his personal investigations on the two-dimensional plane. The architect, on the other hand, uses line in communicating his ideas while the sculptor has much to offer him concerning the understanding of form. The resultant gap between the artist and the architect has paved the way for the colour specialist or consultant who thrives on the neglect by the urban designers of this visual element.

(3) The Artist and Architecture:
The Promise of a New Environmental Colour Tradition

Since the Middle Ages the use of rich architectural colour has sadly declined and the 'fine arts' — painting and sculpture — have followed distinct paths away from the elements of architecture. The few short-lived attempts made to forge links between the artist and the architect have occurred in the present century when a climate became favourable for a dialogue during the Constructivist and Neo-Plasticist movements, and especially in the underlying philosophy of the Bauhaus.

During the simultaneous development of Constructivism in Russia and De Stijl in Holland, relationships between painting, sculpture and architecture changed as painters became concerned with the design of purely abstract volumetric forms. The architectonic nature of these forms was immediately recognized by the new pioneers of urban design and thus, for a time, artistic concepts became transferred to architecture.

The accomplishments of two painters — Kasimir Malevich and Piet Mondrian — contributed significantly to the spatial use of colour, both to internal and external surfaces of buildings. Mondrian's form of Abstraction meant that, for a short period, architectural colour no longer served as an element of decoration but helped to define space. He used only the primary colours — red, blue and yellow against the contrasting tones of white, black and grey. He regarded all other colours as impure, thereby rejecting the browns which had prevailed hitherto, especially in late nineteenth-century interiors.

Perhaps the classic example of the close relationship between artistic and architectural philosophies during this period, is expressed in the Schroder House at Utrecht, designed by Gerrit Rietveld in 1924.

This short-lived 'marriage', with the translation of De Stijl and Constructivist theories into architectural design processes, was not achieved without some conflict. The Russian artist, El Lissitsky, had applauded the new and influential creative forces in art but he also recognized that from this analytical exposure of three-dimensional basic elements had emerged, yet again, two distinct and clearly defined design philosophies: 'That the world is given us through vision, through colour', epitomized one of these views, and 'That the world is given us through touch, through materials', represented the other.

This dualism was to survive the Bauhaus and its attempts to synthesize the plastic arts through their reunification with the design of the built environment. Although principles of colour and colour psychology were introduced into its teaching programme, its brave attack on the traditional Renaissance catagories succumbed, first to intrigues between the art and technological factions of its staff, and finally to Hitler's political purge in 1933.

It seems that when a period of intense involvement with the manipulation of form occurs — as, indeed, has happened in developments of architecture and sculpture — colour considerations become subdued and of relatively reduced importance. This was graphically demonstrated by the Analytical Cubist painters and their two-dimensional investigation into the possibility of a total perspective or all-embracing view of an object. Their activities were so concerned with the organization of synthetic forms that colour became increasingly leaden and almost monochromatic. Conversely, a revival of interest in the singular power of colours, as opposed to their interaction with form, seems to be characterized by a swing towards the bright spectral hues. The decade of the 'swinging sixties' was to see such a movement which was promoted by a young generation rebelling against the colourless urban environment and the monotony of city life. This new sub-culture also expressed itself in pop music and styles of dress when men, as well as women,

28

began to wear brightly coloured garments, breaking an age-old taboo which associated rich colour with effeminacy. The young fashion industry in Britain centred itself in an insignificant back street in London's West End, and the new trend for saturated colour soon became an established part of the façades of Carnaby Street. This colourful street space was soon to become the symbol of the new fashion for colour and style, and still flourishes today.

Although this movement towards brighter colours came as a reaction against the greyness of the post-war period, 'psychedelic' imagery on the outsides of buildings upset some of the city dwellers who, thoroughly conditioned to an austere environment, were emotionally unprepared for intense, exuberant colour in their streets.

Today, a most exciting, and possibly the most promising, trend in the visual arts is the steady erosion of traditional boundaries between the various disciplines and, especially, between painting and sculpture. Artists have become increasingly disenchanted with the strictures of divisional philosophies and their activities began to move away from the search for finite solutions. They now move more freely between media, and seem to be dissolving the 'labels' established during the Renaissance. In 1961 Christo (C. Javacheff) had formed the idea of packaging on an architectural scale. His wrapped buildings and objects, together with the 'happenings' of Alan Kaprow in America and Mark Boyle in England, began to re-establish the fact that art can be a truly public affair by its extension directly into the environment and into our lives.

During the early sixties, the Pop Art movement, with its blurred edges between painting and sculpture, emerged simultaneously in New York and Los Angeles and for its sources drew from the imagery of the mass culture. Its departure from formal channels of art and subject matter heralded the return of colour, in the form of murals and supergraphics, into the street space to take their place next to billboards and traffic signs. The increasing size of Pop Art objects had helped to accelerate the move away from the studio-gallery situation being also accompanied by a growing concern by artists who realized a pressing need to enhance the grey urban environment, and to establish new links with the community by ending their isolation from civic activity.

A notable member of the Pop movement, Alan D'Archangelo, often incorporated real environmental objects into his paintings such as cyclone fencing, road barriers and venetian blinds. In 1967 he was given the opportunity of painting an exterior wall in Manhattan, New York. Excited by the challenge of the scale of this architectural 'canvas', he found this city wall to be a perfect medium for his work.

City Walls Inc. has since produced many such murals in New York City, some of which rise as much as twelve storeys high. The group includes Richard Anuskiewicz, Mel Perkarsky and other artists who, inspired by the ancient use of colour in exterior spaces, promote the introduction of strong, fresh colour into derelict city areas. Doris Freedman, the President of City Walls Inc., claims that the resultant transformations have instilled a new sense of pride in local residents and demonstrated the new possibilities to other artists who are concerned about urban decay (fig. 3).

This new art form, freed from the gallery and the picture frame, must have shocked and surprised many Cincinnatians when the first coloured walls appeared in their city. Here, in contrast to the mainly abstract murals in New York, elements of humour and visual satire are added to the city's landscape. Paul Levy, whose giant painted wing nut and bolt seems to hold together the Cokesbury Bookstore building (fig. 4), sums up the urban painters' attitude: 'In creating a wall painting, one must have as much fun as one can as there are too many gloomy walls in the city centres. The absurd is always the rule. The spectator should be overwhelmed and walk away smiling and remembering . . .'

Sociologists in Cincinnati have watched the projects with some interest. They maintain that in densely populated ghettos where walls have been painted there has been a drop in the crime rate and an increased attendance in community affairs. Their introduction has also added credibility and acceptance to the role of the artist in community planning. Working with city planners, architects and builders he can begin to help relate his expertise to urban areas by employing colour to humanize the built environment. It is also a new medium for him to explore and provides an opportunity to add to, what has been dubbed, 'the quality of life'. This comparatively recent redirection of artistic activity signals the first stage of a promising new development in the urban landscape. Superficially, it represents a simple shift from painting on canvas to the painting of external façades but, more importantly, it heralds a rejection of drab and derelict environments (see fig. 5).

Colour, Competence and Cognition:
Notes Towards a Psychology of Environmental Colour

Dr S. Friedman and Susan Thompson

It appears that the built environment, those objects which are structured by people and surround much of their lives, is glaringly deficient in at least two important respects. These are referred to above as 'competence' and 'cognition' and the environmental situation in regard to them can best be summarized by the two following statements: (1) we are immersed in a physical environment upon which it is very difficult to have any impact; (2) we are immersed in a physical environment which is very difficult to know or understand. It is the major contention of this work that this is not a good situation, and that the creative use of colour in the environment can provide some solutions to these problems.

The term 'competence' was first employed by Robert White (1959) in his work on developmental psychology and personality theory. 'Competence' refers to 'an organism's capacity to interact effectively with its environment' and, in many cases, is based upon the organism's capacity to have impact upon both the social and physical environment. It is White's belief that healthy personality development cannot take place without behaviours of this sort, and a number of other theorists, including Erikson (1950) and Piaget (1950), have stressed the importance of behaviour of this type. The importance of having impact, clearly related to power and the issue of reciprocity in relationships, has been extensively explored in areas as diverse as 'person perception', i.e., the procedures employed in forming images and impressions of other people (Taguiri and Patrillo, 1958), human interaction (Goffman, 1959), and poverty and racism (Ryan, 1971). In a recent work, Robert Sommer develops the idea of 'hard architecture', and one aspect of this type of structure is the difficulty of bringing about any change in the structure. Similarly, in their introduction to the work of O. K. Moore, Friedman and Juhasz (1974) talk of the importance of developing responsive environments, that is, settings upon which individuals can have impact.

There seems to be wide agreement that having impact upon the context is an important component of behaviour and, without it, negative consequences frequently result. At times these negative consequences can be reversed by structuring environments so that the possibility of impact *does* exist. The work of O. K. Moore serves as a good example of this.

Moore has had a remarkable success in motivating and teaching children to read through the use of what he terms an 'autotelic responsive environment'. This is a giant teaching-machine-typewriter-slide-projector which allows the child to directly and dramatically manipulate the learning environment. Children who earlier refused to have anything to do with learning to read became totally involved in the process and would leave only with reluctance when the 'lesson' was over.

Behaviour such as the recent outburst of graffiti in the New York City subway system, the persistent interest bystanders have always had in activities taking place on construction sites, and the appearance in many urban neighbourhoods of large outdoor murals, are *both* evidence of environmental deficiencies in regard to providing contexts upon which people can have impact, *and* examples of possible solutions to this problem. An awareness of the problem on the part of those responsible for the structuring of the environment should result in the creation of additional strategies in dealing with the difficulty.

The term 'cognition' in the title of this work refers to both the activities and operations organisms perform in order to 'know' or 'understand' an object or event, and psychological theories which place such activities and operations at the centre of their explanations of behaviour. There are many such theories and any list generally includes the work of Bartlett (1932), Tolman (1932), George Kelly (1955), Theodore Sarbin (1960), Paul McReynolds (1960), and numerous others who attempt to explain behaviour ranging in diversity from the performance of a rat in a maze to the symptoms of various psychopathologies. The major similarity of all theories which are labelled 'cognitive' is that the organism is assumed to be motivated to want to 'know', and the activities and operations which are performed in this pursuit are seen as central in accounting for all the behaviour of the organism.

Cognitive theories of anxiety (McReynolds, 1960; Sarbin, 1964) generally state that events or objects which individuals cannot schematize, i.e., think about or place within a mental category, are those things which will make individuals anxious and will push them to behave and think in ways which will reduce this anxiety. McReynolds uses a cognitive model to account for much behaviour which is typically thought of as pathological, e.g. the complete withdrawal in certain types of schizophrenia where the individual ceases entirely to interact with the world. Milgram (1970) employs a similar model to account for a number of aspects of urban living, including bystander intervention in crises, norms of civility, and the phenomenon of anonymity. In his pioneering work on environmental perception Kevin Lynch (1960) stresses the importance of 'knowing' the physical environment within which one behaves, and in a similar vein, Goodman and Goodman (1962) mainly base their plea for an enlightened, humanistic, functional design upon the assumption that it is not good for individuals to be surrounded by objects and settings of whose work they have no knowledge.

As stated earlier, it is the belief of the authors that the built environment with which we are surrounded is difficult, if not impossible, for most of us to know, and that this generally leads to negative consequences. Among those negative consequences, cognitive theorists have talked of withdrawal and attention deployment (McReynolds, 1960; Sarbin and Allen, 1968), i.e., diverting attention away from that which is unknowable, and it is interesting to speculate whether widely held anti-urban attitudes (White and White, 1962) are based upon similar dynamics. We don't 'know' the urban environment, so we have negative attitudes to it.

It is interesting to note that those individuals responsible for the structuring of environments—architects, planners and designers—are probably unaware of the failing of physical environments in areas of 'competence' and 'cognition' because they are members of the very groups which are most likely to have these needs met. If you are an urban planner you *can* have impact upon the city and *are* provided with models and concepts which allow you to comprehend, or at least attempt to comprehend, the complexities of physical contexts.

If it is the case, as we have suggested, that people's desire to know, 'cognition', and to have impact, 'competence', are not satisfied in the built environment, two general strategies for reducing this dissatisfaction come to mind. The first of these consists of directly influencing and changing organisms and their behaviour. This can be referred to as a policy solution. Education is one example of this strategy. If people have difficulty knowing and categorizing the built environment, perhaps they can be provided with a more sophisticated category system through the provision of knowledge and information in architecture, design and related fields. Given time and financial restrictions, this becomes more a theoretical than practical solution for many individuals. In the realm of 'competence', advocacy planning and changes in norms of behavioural laws so that individuals can have impact on their environments, in the planning and post-planning stages, exemplify policy solutions.

1
Wall painting on house at St Mande, France designed and painted by Yehiel Rabinowitz. (photo: AOM)

The second general strategy can be called a technological solution and refers to the design of built environments which are both easier to know and easier to have impact upon. Although colour can be a part of a policy solution, e.g. changing dormitory rules so that students can paint their rooms any colour they desire, in most examples which come to mind, colour is used as part of a technological solution.

In discussing these examples, it is important to note that although the two dimensions of 'cognition' and 'competence' have been presented as if they were independent of each other, in actual practice this is not always the case. Frequently, knowing and understanding an environment is a necessary precondition of having impact upon it, and conversely, the process and products of having impact upon an environment enable us to know it more fully.

The Boston Freedom Trail is a good example of an ordering device imposed on a physical environment which helps facilitate a cognitive understanding of that environment. By following red footsteps painted on the streets of Boston, the participant is led past Paul Revere's house, the Old North Church, and many other historical monuments of colonial Boston. A confusing maze of streets has been simply and effectively converted to a more positive experience without reducing any of the complexity which adds to the delight of the experience.

Colour-coding has been employed in a variety of settings including old age homes, machine rooms of office buildings, and primary schools. In the latter, the hope is that the children will come to understand the environment where their education is taking place. This seems particularly appropriate in a physical setting where the value of knowledge is continuously stressed. The child comes to know its environment through the use of colour, and also has a definite message conveyed to it about the nature of the learning process and the comprehensibility of the environment. In addition to the positive effects bright colour introduces into the previously sterile classroom environment, the painting of environmental components draws attention to these components, demanding that the child utilize them as elements for learning. Colour and object are united, each being primary to the understanding of the environment.

The importance of having impact on the physical environment through the use of colour has become an increasing concern of a number of contemporary visual artists. The American painter, Gene Davis, famous for his acrylic stripe canvases, recently executed a work at the Philadelphia Museum of Art where he painted the driveway leading to the museum with his characteristic stripe signature (fig. 6). Besides acting as a focal point for the museum façade itself, this work both reflects the growing demand that artists be allowed greater freedom in determining how their work will be exhibited, and is a vivid example of the impact of colour.

Our last example illustrates a number of things which have been implicit in much of what was said above. As stated earlier, there has been a resurgence in interest in large outdoor murals in many urban neighbourhoods. These works are graphic examples of members of communities having impact upon their physical contexts and also frequently help meet people's cognitive needs. The meeting of these cognitive needs is accomplished in a variety of ways ranging from the possibility that the content or subject matter of the mural can provide useful information about the neighbourhood, its history, spatial arrangement, etc., to the very presence of the mural acting as a distinctive landmark which helps people to orient themselves spatially.

These outdoor murals also serve as good examples of a number of advantages of using colour as a solution to the environmental problems of 'cognition' and 'competence'. In general, they are relatively inexpensive, easily amenable to change, and allow the participation of a wider range of individuals than is typical in most urban environmental changes of this scale.

The Future Role of the Artist

Victor Vasarely

For decades the creative act has been surrounded by a mystique which is as nebulous as it is ambiguous. This confusion has been deliberately perpetuated by the exponents of metaphysical and transcendental art; it has acted as a supplementary means for ensuring that art should preserve its esoteric character and for its retention as the property of a cultured minority. The time is approaching for the end of this kind of personal art for a sophisticated elite, especially in an era where our civilization is being controlled by the techniques of science.

In order to live, man needs plastic beauty just as much as he needs oxygen and vitamins. It is up to the artist to provide this but within the context of the total environment. To accomplish this end he must abandon the idea of the single poetic function together with the myth of the painted object, and dare at last to undertake his integration into the design processes of the built environment as only through collaborating with scientific research and technical disciplines will he truly create.

The coding in a square of the 'form-colour units' (fig. 7) confers the maximum flexibility for handling them in compositions, with a rigorously arithmetical possibility of reference as the base. The unit has two constants: the core 'form' and its complement which surrounds it—the square 'background'. Apart from its two-form aspect, it necessarily has a two-colour aspect (harmonious and contrasted and, at the same time, positive-negative). With an alphabet of thirty forms and a range of thirty colours, we already have several thousand possible combinations by the mere interchanging of the pairs ... According to the number of units included in a composition, as a result of more complex interchanges by using progressive sizes (mixing in the same composition units two, four, eight or sixteen times bigger), the number of possibilities reaches an inexpressible, practically infinite figure. The appearance in the plastic arts of a combination of this range provides a tool with a universal character, while at the same time permitting the manifestation of personality, as well as that of ethnic particularisms. One already perceives the contours of a genuine 'planetary folklore', modern in its idea and its technique, unitary at its base and highly complex at its summits.

The integration into architecture by virtue of this reaches the operational phase: the industrial manufacture of plastic units is possible in the form of elements of every material, of every colour and every size. This technique of embellishment, intrinsic with the function, enables us to glimpse the polychrome city.

The form-colour unit, being an immense reservoir of harmonizing or exalting stimuli, opens up prospects of health and joy needed for the equilibrium of vast concentrations of human beings.

Overleaf:

2
Section of painted exterior frieze from the east side of the Parthenon — colour reconstruction by the Royal Ontario Museum, Toronto. (Photo: copyright Rom.)

3
Untitled city wall designed by Mel Pekarsky for a façade at Houston and Crosby Streets, Manhattan, New York.

4
Giant wing nut and bolt. Cincinnati urban wall designed by Paul Levy.

5
Elements of humour and visual satire are added to Cincinnati's urban landscape by Barron Krody's 'fluttering' Stars and Stripes.

6
Gene Davis working on his floorscape painting *Franklin's Footpath* installed on the parkway approach to the Philadelphia Museum of Art.

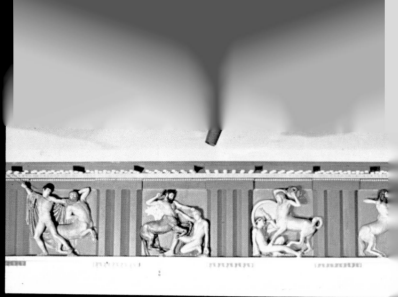

5

3

3   The Functions of Colour in Architectural Settings

'As early as 1910, I knew about the bracing quality of chalk white. Practice showed me that the joy of white explodes only when surrounded by the powerful hum of colour.' Le Corbusier

Apart from the traditional and widespread use of naturally coloured building materials, the function of pigment and paint in external architectural space is varied. Its presence sometimes stems from the conscious manipulation of colour as part of the architect's design process but, more often, it is applied as an afterthought in the form of a protective or decorative skin. Coloured pigment has in some cases been added to modern construction materials in an attempt to integrate dominant man-made forms into their settings. In this manner, colour can be utilized as a unifying device in the merging of architectural mass with the predominating features of a natural or built landscape.

For example, the concrete shell of Ioh Ming Pei's Upper Atmosphere Observatory, which is magnificently sited in the Colorado Rockies, was colour-matched through the addition of pigment to the colour of the mountain stone found in that region. Similarly, the tinted concrete of the Nuffield Transplantation Surgery Unit by Peter Womersley in Edinburgh attempts a colour-match with the golden-brown brick façades of near-by houses. Both of these comparatively recent examples illustrate the architect's desire to reduce the intrusion of their buildings and reflects the natural integration process of the smaller-scale traditional rural architecture whose forms, being constructed from local materials, mirror the colours of their location.

A further example of colour blending, but in this case to a specific point in time, is illustrated by the Golden Gate bridge in San Francisco. The suspension bridge was, in fact, originally planned as a symbolic golden structure and a monument to the 1849 gold rush. The scheme was later modified, however, and its existing oxide red hue is intended to colour-match the bedrock on each side of the bay.

The environmental colour programmes of the French 'coloriste', Jean-Philippe Lenclos, have produced some wide-ranging but essentially positive colour contributions to the man-made landscape. Lenclos's pioneer work is the first major attempt to endow the built landscape with richly coloured space and represents an exciting and 'painterly' approach affording a glimpse of the future potential of environmental colour embodied in the philosophies of Léger and Vasarely. His colour applications range from the collaboration with architects on individual buildings to the development of a comprehensive grammar of polychromy for new towns.

At Port Barcares near Perpignan, by using supergraphics, Lenclos transformed a large marine industrial building into a giant signboard which echoes the colours of the sea in much the same way as the fishermen's houses in Brittany reflect the colours of their boats (fig. 11). In another industrial colour programme he reversed this process and adopted a *palette d'integration* to minimize the four main towers of a cement plant situated at Mantes near Paris. In the attempt to integrate this dominant industrial form into the landscape, three horizontal coloured bands were introduced to the cylindrical towers; the base section being painted blue in order to create a link with the surrounding hills (fig. 51). At La Ciotat, a small port near Marseilles, Lenclos prescribed the dockside cranes to be painted in the exact colour of the stone fabric of the near-by town as a means of reducing the visual conflict between mechanical and domestic forms (fig. 52).

The opposite of this assimilation process can also occur. Exuberant colour has always followed periods of austerity, and is often applied to contrast with monochromatic or dismal surroundings or to re-establish an identity. The tower block 'Ichi Ban Kahn' in Shinjuku, a suburb of Tokyo — painted by architect Minoru Takeyama — challenges its encompassing squalor through a highly saturated red, yellow and blue. Similarly, Jacques Starkier, the French architect, has explained how he attacked the pervading greyness of Levallois-Perret with a red, orange and yellow elementary school building which provides the children of the Parisian suburb with a personal 'possession'. Another French school by architect Georges Pencreac'h located in the new town of Cergy Pontoise demonstrates the effects of consultant Lenclos's exuberant manipulation of colour, which both reflects the sheer enjoyment of rich, saturated colour by the young and boosts the visual impact of the area and its architecture (figs. 8 and 10).

Colour can also humanize industrial environments. The colour programmes devised by Lenclos for gigantic machinery and industrial architecture are attempts to help man come to terms with the machine environment (fig. 53). (Later, Lenclos explains how this humanizing process can also be applied to the urban landscape.)

As a decorative element, colour has also been applied by designers to fragment or 'destroy' the visual rectilinearity of modern architectural mass. This principle was adopted by the Italian architect, Carlo Santi, in a housing project in Bologna. His curved, multi-coloured shapes rendered on to the exterior walls, being totally at variance with the structure, resemble Eduardo Paolozzi's application of colour to disrupt the angularity of his sculpted forms. However, more recent development of 'colour camouflage' seeks only to conceal anonymous architecture through a contrasting interplay of colour and form which attacks monotonous space in a striking and sometimes humorous fashion.

The annual ritual of housepainting in the villages of Greek islands, particularly

Overleaf:

7
Victor Vasarely, *Orion-MC,* 1964. Oil on canvas 189 × 180 cm. Collection: The Vasarely Didactic Museum at Gordes, Vaucluse.

8
Les Maradas School, Cergy Pontoise. Lenclos's colour prescription picks out protruding forms around the building in a spectral sequence. (photo: Jacques Dirand)

9
Detail of school (Ecole de la Haye aux Moines) at Créteil, France, designed by J. C. Bernard. Colour by Jean-Philippe Lenclos. (photo: J.-Ph. Lenclos)

10
Les Maradas School. Colour penetrates through to the interior circulation spaces. (photo: J.-Ph. Lenclos)

11
Painted supergraphic by Jean-Philippe Lenclos on an industrial building at the naval shipyard of Port Barcares near Perpignan. (photo: F. Puyplat)

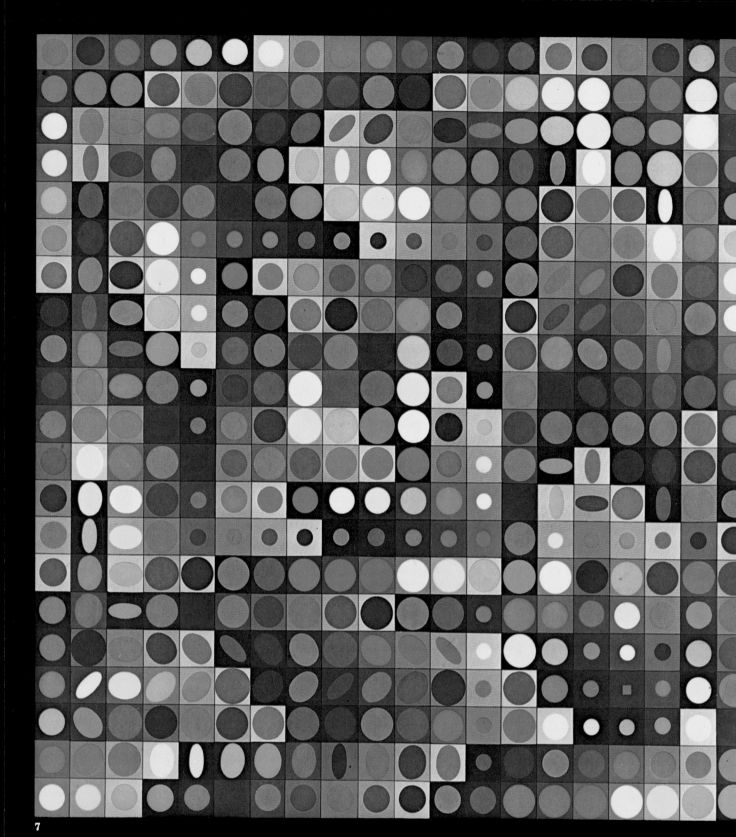

7

8

9

10

11

Crete and Rhodes, expresses a kind of rebirth through the redefining of territory and identity. In this traditional context, colour acts as a personal signature in the punctuation of secondary elements in the façades of houses — in much the same way as colour washes were applied to the columns and pediments at Knossos. This exploitation and enjoyment of colour as a dimension for changing the appearance of external space can be found in many parts of the world, particularly in South America where, as in Greece, simple but essentially rich colour combinations are haphazardly juxtaposed with little conscious consideration for harmonious relationships. These environments are constantly changing, not only through the effect of colour but also by its physical presence: successive layers of paint and limewash gradually blurring the forms and softening the transition between house and street.

This positive identification of important architectural elements provides an opportunity of incorporating both a rich variety of colour together with a corresponding variety of spatial effects into the built environment. However, although colour has been used more frequently in this manner as part of the modern architectural vocabulary, the results are often frugal as they are generated from a badly digested functionalism and a rigorous concern for 'necessary' architecture. In this context, colour connotes superficiality and frivolity.

Clearly defined colour, as an organizational and informational aspect of architectural expression in public and external spaces, can provide an unambiguous structure which is able to reduce apprehension in complex, large-scale or totally artificial environments. This form of architectural expression has obvious roots in the philosophies of the Constructivists, Neo-Plasticists, and Purists. Le Corbusier, who was an artist member of the latter group, developed and refined this approach in his design process and, in a paper written for students entitled 'If I Had to Teach Architects', he said: 'Here is a golden rule. Use coloured pencils. With colour you accentuate, you classify, you disentangle. With black you get stuck in the mud and you are lost. Always say to yourself: *Drawings must be easy to read*. Colour will come to your rescue.'

Sadly, a dynamic colour programme has not been called to the rescue of the modern environment. This is strange, however, because most architects use adjectives such as 'feeling' and 'character' to describe the visual impressions of their spaces, and these collective terms represent the sum total of the visual components contained both within their design vocabulary and within their immediate control. These include colour, light, form, texture and pattern and are those very components which unite him with the artist. The use of the words 'feeling' and 'character' underlines the necessity to consider the interaction of these visual forces so that manifestations of design concepts achieve a balanced orchestration and an appropriate relationship to specific spatial contexts. It also becomes apparent that, if colour is to take on a more positive role in the design process, architectural form must anticipate its function and be sympathetically related to its organization.

Thus far we have underlined the lack of conscious colour use in environmental design and studied the various reasons which might have prompted this dilemma. However, there is evidence of a return by some architects to colour, as if to a primordial element. Men such as Joseph Esherick and Oscar Newman in America, Jean Deroche in France, Norman Foster and Piano and Rogers in England are now attempting to endow the landscape with coloured spaces in the recognition that colour is not only an aesthetic force but also a language.

They have kindly contributed statements to this chapter. As they are concerned particularly with their colour approach in designing for the built environment and are presented together with statements from artists involved in environmental design, they might begin to narrow the gulf between the hitherto separate philosophies of the artist and the architect.

Colour as a Function of Multi-Dimensional Space:
A New Architecture of Urban Environment

Victor Pasmore

One of the principle features of the revolution in the visual arts of the twentieth century is the freedom and independence of colour. The most positive manifestation of this has been in painting in which works of such artists as Bonnard, Léger, Matisse, Miró, Mondrian and Picasso have been the leading examples. But, whereas the revolution in painting has been total, in the sense that it has embraced also form, image and technique, the one in architecture has not included colour. New building techniques such as tensile construction and curtain-walling, coupled with new materials, have enabled the architect to achieve a new image of space and volume, but as yet no positive approach has been made in terms of colour. But although maintainance problems have obviously been an inhibiting factor, the causes of this restraint are not entirely technical. The functionalist philosophy, on which architecture based its modern revolution, concentrated on objective factors, like utility and technology, with the result that subjective functions, like that of colour, were overlooked. Moreover, except in multi-storey blocks, the use of natural material is still the dominant factor in urban building which means that its tertiary tones will inevitably set the key to any concept of architectural colour over a large area. However, if dependence on synthetic material and prefabricated construction continues to increase at the present rate, then architecture will finally lose all its basic natural connections except in marginal form. Out altogether, therefore, will go the country town clinging to a hillside or nestling in a valley with its walls built of the natural stone on which it stands and the timber by which it is surrounded. Prefabrication and synthetic material make such an intimate relationship out of the question. It is this increasing erosion of naturalism in building construction which leaves the door open for a colour revolution in architecture.

But there are other more sophisticated reasons for a new approach to the use of colour in architecture — reasons which are connected with the concept and structure of space. Architecture is essentially an aesthetic of space as well as of construction in mass; this is because architectural form was derived originally from the building of

Overleaf:

12
Swimming stadium at Chatillon-sur-Seine by AUA architects Jean and Maria Deroche with Paul Chemitov. Mural by Mariano Hernandez. (photo: Jean Pierre Buel)

13
Rendered colour transformation at Clason Point in the Bronx, New York City, Oscar Newman.

14
R. Desnos Secondary School at Orly, Paris. Colour by the architects, Jean and Maria Deroche. (photo: Michel Desjardins)

15
Cal Poly Union Building, San Luis Obispo, designed by Esherick, Homsey, Dodge and Davis. (photo: K. Kershaw)

16
Banneker Homes at San Francisco, designed by Esherick, Homsey, Dodge and Davis. (photo: K. Kershaw)

17
Banneker Homes (photo: K. Kershaw)

18
Interior of BART station at San Leandro, designed by Esherick, Homsey, Dodge and Davis. (photo: K. Kershaw)

19
San Leandro BART station (photo: K. Kershaw)

20
Entrance to BART station at Lafayette. (photo: K. Kershaw)

12

14

13

15 16 17

20

habitable dwellings or caves. As a human dwelling, a building encloses within its walls a section of natural space. Once a group of such enclosures is erected, they form a network not only of solid spatial enclosures, but also of exterior connecting spaces. It is this multiple spatial construction which constitutes the architecture of urban environment. However, before considering a function for colour in this context, it is necessary to take into account the differences between the modern and classical concepts of space. This difference is signified by the term 'multi-dimensions'. But in fact the multi-dimensional concepts which the visual arts have adapted from modern scientific theory involve practical problems which cannot be resolved in terms of concrete building without the aid of subjective means; that is to say, by optical or psychological effects. This means the introduction of a new form of 'perspective' by which the concrete three-dimensional structure of buildings is fragmented or 'exploded' by subjecting it to optical ambiguity. In other words, the urban architect would have to do what the Cubists initiated in painting. It is in this 'impressionist' sense that free and independent colour might play a part in realizing the multi-dimensional concept of urban environment.

That the use of colour in this way and on an urban scale would involve serious problems, both technical and psychological, is obvious, because there could be no question of collective repetition or concentrated individualization. Moreover, building units would have to be specially designed with panels set at different levels and angles which could be freely coloured either by the architect or by the occupier. Indeed, a multi-coloured architectural environment would only be dynamic if it comprised a mixture of collective planning and individual enterprise as in the case of night-lighting in cities. Here, perhaps, is the basic example. One has only to fly over London on a clear night or view the lights of New York from one of its skyscrapers to see how free and independent colour, artificially constructed, can transform a grey and concrete town into a magical experience.

The Use of Colour and Texture at Clason Point

Oscar Newman

In my work in America I have noticed that most of the successful practising architects were trained at our Ivy League schools: Harvard, Yale, Princeton, M.I.T. They appear also to have been educated in a Bauhaus tradition which relies heavily on the use of three-dimensional grey cardboard models in the design process. These models intentionally refrain from any display of materials, colours or textures. As a representation of actual environments, the models are more severe than anything we can build. The literal translation of these models into buildings would produce a raw concrete surface both inside and out. Raw concrete, although satisfying the purist aesthetic of the modern architect, is a material which is alien to the tastes of most of the buildings' users.

Most people enjoy variations in the colour and texture of natural materials in the environments they inhabit — particularly in their homes. Richly textured and coloured environments are not only rewarding to the sight and touch but they are perceived by many as an expression of affluence — or gratification in the form of conspicuous consumption.

The capacity to enjoy the purity and severity of raw concrete is a predilection of only the most sophisticated in our society. Low and middle-income people usually associate the austerity of raw concrete with bunkers and prisons. A very wealthy client by contrast may share the tastes and values of the architect and may find status rewards in living in buildings which represent the most avant-garde of current architectural idioms. If an architect's clients have had money in the family for a long enough time, they may be sufficiently self-assured to be able to perceive raw concrete as representing high style and the most current fashion. Most of the *nouveaux riches* are not that self-assured.

There is a ladder of taste among different income groups in our society which parallels class structure. The lowest rung of the ladder would parallel the lowest income group in society and the highest rung, the richest in the society. One finds that the artifacts that each class chooses to surround itself with and to define its status are the objects they perceive as representative of the environments of the class immediately above them, that is to say, the class to which they aspire. People select and choose objects and housing which they see in use by the people in the class above them. Ironically, the objects may not be in current vogue with that class because they in turn have higher aspirations. Inevitably, of course, what each is able to afford for itself is the less expensive reproduction of the artifacts of the class above. The point, though, is that few aspire to the tastes of those of the rich on the second to the top rung of the ladder. The very top rung of the ladder is occupied by the architect-tastemaker, just above the only class in society which shares his values. It is to the group of the very rich immediately below him that the architect is most important as it is to this group that keeping up with the most current vogue is most necessary.

Lee Rainwater, an American sociologist, recognized another phenomenon, that is that with increased income there is a cumulative effect on the number of criteria to be satisfied in housing. The poorest in our societies are primarily concerned with shelter: from weather, rodents, insects, and other people. The working class add to

21
'A synthesis of architecture, painting and sculpture — having no utilitarian function.' Detail of pavilion and mural at Peterlee designed by Victor Pasmore in conjunction with A. T. W. Marsden, Chief Architect, Peterlee, set against the dark umber brickwork and painted timber panelling of the housing in the south-west area. (photo: John Pasmore)

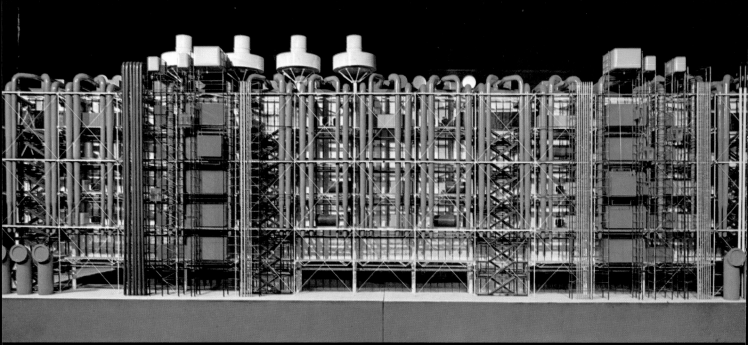

22

23

these basic requirements a certain need for cosiness. The middle class add expanded spatial requirements — and some concern for materials and colour. The upper-middle class requires that all this be assembled with some style. Finally, the very rich require that the assembly be in current or chic style. The function of television in defining values and tastes and in creating aspirations is not to be minimized. Our own findings suggest that even though the need for primitive shelter may be the dominant concern for the lowest income groups that this group is nevertheless very conscious of colour, texture and 'appearances'.

I became very conscious of the operation of these mechanisms when I became involved in the construction and modification of a few public housing projects. I was astounded, in our Institute's survey of residents in housing both in the United States and Britain, at the differences between architects' tastes and the tastes of their clients. This was evidenced by the incredible contrast in the colours, materials and textures used by residents in decorating the inside of their own apartments compared with surfaces of the buildings outside their apartments. Within the realms under their control residents had produced colourfully decorated environments — not necessarily at great cost. Outside was a world that the architect designed. Raw concrete was the prevalent material; grey and off-white the dominant

(Above left:)
22
Architecture as a colourful urban machine: model of Centre Beaubourg, Paris, showing the rue du Renard elevation with vinyl coated service systems. Piano and Rogers. (photo: Bernard Vincent)
23 *(Below left:)*
A factory for UOP Fragrances at Tadworth, Surrey, designed by Piano and Rogers. (photo: Richard Einzig)

(Overleaf)
24
Ricardo Bofill's La Muralla Roja (red wall) at Sitges in the bay of Calpe, Spain.
25
Detail from La Muralla Roja.
26
Barrio Gaudi (Gaudi Quarter) housing at Reus, Tarragona.
27
Barrio Gaudi detail.
'Architecture may be understood as the physical materialization of a concept, of a way of living.
'The most important thing in architecture is space; organized by the volumes and surfaces that limit it.
'We conceive the organization of this space within certain criteria and a systemization which is different and individual for each project. They are functions of the form itself.
'The formal laws are geometrical, but then comes the problem of the treatment of the "Skin" — that which covers the volumes, with all its range of beams, 'angles, lintels, etc., and which constitutes the more subjective and expressive side of architecture.
'Colour should be used to underline the internal laws of the architectonic form of the building and to make it visible and artistic.
'Colour is not only paint, but also the texture of the material employed: brick, stone, concrete . . .
'Through colour, architecture can be brought to life, a living breath to animate the coldness of the building.
'With respect to the building, colour can either serve as make-up, overlaying the structure, or it can restrain itself in the interests of the architecture and serve to emphasize it. supporting the conformation of the diverse spaces.
'With respect to the surroundings, colour can be used to harmonize with the landscape or townscape, either as camouflage or as a contrast to the surroundings achieving harmony by confrontation.
'There is no architecture without colour; even when it is omitted, it is still there.'
Anna and Ricardo Bofill
28
Schweizer's colour wheel. The outer ring contains seven colour ranges for doors and details; the inner ring contains the range of basic façade colours. The residents of Hoechst were invited by Schweizer to select colour combinations by rotating the outer wheel in order to integrate detail colours with the chosen façade colour.
29
Coloured patent rendering on the medieval façades of Hoechst, Germany. The colour scheme was co-ordinated by Gerhard Schweizer in participation with the area residents.
30
Another view of the medieval façades of Hoechst.

24

26

25

27

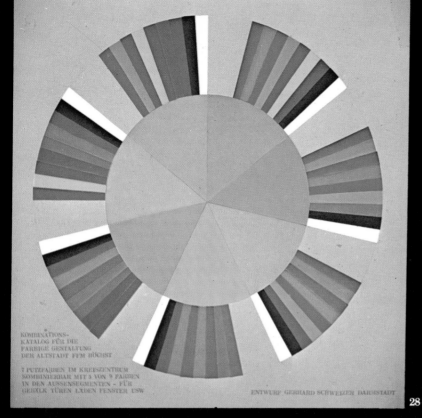

KOMBINATIONS-
KATALOG FÜR DIE
FARBIGE GESTALTUNG
DER ALTSTADT FFM HÖCHST

7 PUTZFARBEN IM KREISZENTRUM
KOMBINIERBAR MIT 3 VON 9 FARBEN
IN DEN AUSSENSEGMENTEN - FÜR
GEBÄLK TÜREN LÄDEN FENSTER USW

ENTWURF GERHARD SCHWEIZER DARMSTADT

28

29

30

colour. Only the glass areas occasionally broke up the drabness by reflecting a blue sky.

Although one might be led to believe that the absence of varied materials and colours on the surfaces of the buildings is the result of an inadequate budget, in fact, it is more the result of the tastes and preferences of the architect. It takes a strong-minded resident indeed not to succumb to the depressive world of raw concrete around him and find the energy and inspiration to create for himself a different world within his apartment.

As an architect in New York I was given the opportunity to modify the grounds and façades of a low-income housing project built of grey cement block. The weather penetration and heat loss through the cement block was so great, that the Housing Authority decided to cover the block with three coats of cement. I used this as an opportunity to go beyond this basic functional requirement and add both colour and texture to the surface of the buildings and the grounds of the project.

My ideas for upgrading this housing project were derived from observations of what middle-income residents, living in uniform row-house blocks, do to enrich and individualize their homes. They add surface colours, shutters and awnings. I persuaded the contractor carrying out the work to consider varying the colours in his final coat of cement and then to score the final cement coat so that it would have the appearance of brickwork. I selected eight possible colours for the façades of Clason Point and had the contractor prepare a sample wall on site to demonstrate to the residents the system of application and the range of colours available. We also produced a colour chart which illustrated possible colour combinations. Although each unit would have its own colour we suggested that only two colours be used for each row-house block. Residents had to get together with their neighbours to co-ordinate their colour selections. I had to relax the restrictions on colour combinations later when residents reacted negatively to some of my more conservative suggested colour combinations.

The contractor estimated that the additional colours and scoring work would add 25 per cent to the cost of the cement finish. I suggested to the Housing Authority that the cost would be worth it, in that it would produce a radically different environment — one which residents would take pride in and which would stimulate them to undertake their own decorating and maintenance of their buildings and grounds. I was aided in my efforts by the Chairman of the New York City Housing Authority, a black attorney whose education and success had apparently not blocked his memory to the values and tastes of low-income populations. The initial building which the contractor prepared on an experimental basis produced such an incredibly different mood and atmosphere that we were able to convince the Chairman and the Board members who came to see it to provide the additional funds necessary.

The Clason Point project was an experiment aimed at determining if people would respond to external, superficial changes made to their environment. The test results prove most fascinating. Not only did people respond by painting their own doors and windows in the first year — but in subsequent years they made extensive improvements to their gardens and to the interiors of their houses. Rich colours and materials began to appear on the grounds and insides of apartment units. By 'rich' I do not mean 'expensive' (fig. 13).

Our contractor also told us that where at the beginning of construction his equipment was being so vandalized that he felt it necessary to remove it each evening, but as soon as the effect of our modifications became more apparent he found that the nocturnal abuse to his equipment had ceased.

Subsequent in-depth interviews with residents demonstrated that people were very conscious indeed of colour and texture (Kohn, Franck, Fox, 'Defensible Space Modifications in Row-House Communities', Institute for Community Design

Analysis, Inc., New York, 1975). They valued the changes to the building façades more highly than either the new lighting, benching or fencing provided. The low-income residents were also found to be very articulate on the subject of colour and texture and knew exactly what they wanted their immediate environments to look like. They were very clear about their likes and dislikes. And their tastes are completely at variance with the tastes and values acquired by architects in school.

Much of contemporary architectural education is actually a form of brain-washing. I remember a student of mine at Columbia University, returning to the School of Architecture after a summer's recess, saying that he had not realized before how bad were the tastes of his parents. In the pursuit of our own aesthetic we have, as architects and educators, succeeded in estranging ourselves and our students from the tastes, values and aesthetic aspirations of most of society.

Our work at Clason Point is being strongly criticized by the architectural profession. Many see it as little more than stage-set design — and kitsch stage-set at that. They say that I have catered to the lowest level of taste amongst the residents, and that, as an architect I have the responsibility to elevate the tastes of my clients. I can imagine that there are many architects who would have used a single, uniform, subdued colour for the entire project. Our interviewing revealed how strongly the residents appreciated and responded to the rich and varied colour of their new environment. Surely there must be some way we can satisfy the tastes and needs of our client-groups while still satisfying our own professional tastes and aspirations. If architects need insight and direction into people's preferences let them look at how people decorate and colour what is their own: the insides of their homes and apartments.

(Overleaf:)
31
Bright buildings in a neutral landscape: blue warehouse for Modern Art Glass Ltd on an industrial landscape at Thamesmead, London. (photo: Foster Associates)
32
Internal use of colour to diagram the building structure: windowless interior of the SAPA (Scandinavian Aluminium Profiles AB) extrusion plant enlivened by the use of bright colours on machinery and structure. (photo: Foster Associates)
33
Airtent project at Hemel Hempstead, Herts., for Computer Technology Ltd. (photo: Foster Associates)
34
Perception of environment: a bright red carpet was used to 'warm' the perception of changing environmental conditions inside the unheated pneumatic structure. (photo: Foster Associates)
35
Window of Standard Shoes Store, Los Angeles, Deborah Sussman and Co.
36
Standard Shoes logo and sign, Los Angeles, Deborah Sussman and Co.
37
Interior, Standard Shoes Store, Los Angeles, Deborah Sussman and Co.
38
Temporary sign, Mexico City.
39
Entrance canopy, Zodys Department store, Los Angeles, Deborah Sussman and Co.

31

32

33

34

36

39

The Temptation of Colour: A Legitimate Attitude for an Architect

Jean Deroche

In our own use of colour we have developed three basic approaches. Let me explain:

First, the enlivening of architecture by colour might come from a collaboration with a painter who, by his intervention, brings into play a painted 'work' which exists in its own right. It is a fascinating matter — difficult but very rewarding. For example, we had to design for a suburban area — a sad and mediocre landscape which was to feature a building important to the whole life of the district. We decided for a shock effect by making a bold statement which used the nature of the surroundings to set it off. Another example is our Nautical Stadium at Chatillon (fig. 12) where the coloration of the gables and screen walls serves as a background to the new architecture. Here the collaboration of the painter, Mariano Hernandez, was a vital contribution.

On the subject of artist and architecture, we are very aware of the delicacy of the problem and the solutions which often miss the desired result. In connection with this I can give two examples: Dieppe town council called in Vasarely to colour a water tower which dominated the entrance to the town's built-up area. The invitation was justified as Vasarely's theories on the polychrome city are well-known in France, but the result was startling, for only a very small part was coloured and the main form was painted grey — the painter had hung up his painting which was nothing more than easel painting for the drawing room. The second example is perhaps even more indicative of the dangers of this approach. It is an older example but concerns a work done in collaboration with one who, perhaps from the point of view of monumental work and particularly of colour, has made the greatest impact on the twentieth century. I am speaking of Fernand Léger, who was invited to work on the exterior of a famous building of post-war France — the Memorial Hospital of St Lo by architects Nelson, Gilbert and Sebillotte.

Léger's proposal, as one might expect, took into consideration the whole of the building, but it broke down its volumes by using coloured areas of simple geometric shapes. This was all the more astonishing as the architecture itself was very cubist, strongly marked by the rationalist tradition and, therefore, close to Léger's own sensibilities.

Our second type of approach was made together with the colour consultant, Max Soumagnac. Integration with the natural landscape was fundamental to the scheme. Our use of colour on the façades of the holiday villages of Grasse and Gassin (both in Provence) followed a desire to respect both tradition and landscape. This produced continuity as well as a means of clearly conveying to the numerous users, who had modest means and conventional cultural ideals, the desire to capture a spirit and to produce a correct scale. All of this was done without any concession, without pastiche, and the architecture was in both cases violently brutal.

Finally, a third colour experiment can be illustrated by a school we designed and recently constructed for the municipality of Orly. Here, as at Chatillon, the setting was inimical but very different in terms of scale: a 'great ensemble' of multi-storey blocks. The architecture and method of construction for this project was chosen not only with regard to the surroundings but also with regard to the user — adolescents who are strongly impressed by modernity and a taste for speed and mechanical devices.

Unlike the preceding instances, we undertook the colour schemes for this building as this was the very essence of the design (fig. 14).

The reactions of the colourist and the architect to the problem of colour in architecture are very different. In our opinion, we architects tend to reason essentially from a functional and constructional reduction to fundamentals, to which didacticism is no stranger. The colourist working with us, however, has always given the impression of working in planes and volumes in creating a surrounding 'atmosphere', but also bringing another dimension to the built space by making it simple or complex. Both approaches seem to be useful even if they are different and ultimately opposed.

For every problem and for every aim there is a correspondingly satisfactory answer — sometimes excluding all others but basically identical in motive, i.e., to make colour or colouring play a full part in the built work and to create a more coherent and more intelligible environment. The success can be tested by its result and its own evidence. One question suffices as a check — would the built space be changed, would it be poorer if the colour was suppressed? and if it were to be suppressed, what would be the reaction of the people living there?

Colour in Buildings

Joseph Esherick

Colour in the 'natural' world, the world of animals, insects, plants and fish, is used in a purposeful and functional way. Man, on the other hand, appears to be burdened by having to think about colour, to study it, to make an issue of it, to design and plan for its use. Scientific studies of colour and light, while important and essential, can either become a crutch to support a lack of conviction or imagination, or an added complexity that makes the commonsense and straightforward use of colour even more difficult.

Designing with colour is easier if one thinks of colour and light together, as essentially inseparable elements. Colour and light are such integral parts of our everyday life and so important to anything we design that it seems odd that one should have to argue for more extensive, more imaginative and more productive uses. Colour and light can be used to give direction, to warn or call attention to an object or event, to modify or change a structure (even to destroy that structure visually), to establish a desired environment, for sheer physical relief, or simply for pleasure and enjoyment.

A first step in an expanded and more effective use of colour is simply to *see* colour and all its subtlety wherever it may be, particularly in the natural world. There is no better way to learn to see something than by trying to reproduce an image of that thing and this means drawing and painting. Photography simply won't do it; one just ends up with a coloured photograph. Architectural and design schools years ago had a much heavier emphasis on work in colour in the drawing and painting studios. Often this work involved painting such objects as subtle porcelains—an entirely different experience from the more modern approach of pasting coloured papers on cubes.

One cannot learn how to use colour by a set of isolated or abstract exercises; one simply has to use it in real world cases and then complete sensible feedback loops by observing the effects. Just as one learns how to use light in buildings and to think of it as an integral part early on in the process, so one should conceive colour. Clearly the colour sketches in the studio are no more the colours to be used in the final structure than the drawings of the building *are* the final structure. It would be the rarest of cases if a studio light environment were identical with the project light environment. Final decisions can only be made on site, under conditions simulating ultimate use with some representation of surrounding components in place. The client or user must be brought into the process as early as possible and he must stay with it through to completion.

In our practice we use colour constantly in our sketches and drawings from the very earliest work through to final designs. We suggest colours diagrammatically on the first schematic ideas and then begin to work towards increasingly specific colour ideas as the work progresses. The client is thus brought along with the notion that colour is significant and we mutually develop a feeling about what colours are more appropriate. For reasons that are not entirely clear to me, we don't seem to think of colour and pattern in the sense of broken-up patterns on a surface but conceive of colour as the surfaces of volumes or the ends of spaces, and always in relation to light. The process is one of continual development and refinement of the ideas; only our construction documents for the building trade are black and white.

College Union, California Polytechnic State University, San Luis Obispo (fig. 15)
When the College Union was being designed campus regulations stringently limited the exterior materials of the building to a particular brick colour and to concrete

58

painted an aimless and undistinguished yellowish tan. During the earlier design stages a rough notion of the interior colours was conceived (of both applied and integral colours) but it was assumed that nothing could be done with the exterior. Just as the building was being completed the authorities made a major change in their regulations and requested the architects to consider leaving the concrete neutral. Since it had not been even vaguely contemplated that the concrete might remain unpainted, no attention was paid to the control of the concrete colour which had the characteristic cold bluish grey of most Californian cements and aggregates.

We felt that colour was extremely important in the grey coastal environment of San Luis Obispo. We knew we did not have the funds for a strong and varied colour programme for the entire building, so we devised a scheme of strong colours mostly orientated towards the inner, more private, plaza of the building — the 'watermelon idea'.

With the change in administration regulations went a perhaps unrelated change in the character of the student body which became less conservative in its views. A few of the older, more conservative students then leaving the campus were outspoken in their antagonism towards the colour but the majority of the students then and to this day are enthusiastic and usually mention it when describing or commenting on the building.

Banneker Homes (figs. 16 and 17)
Banneker Homes is a low-rent housing project in a major redevelopment area in San Francisco. The surrounding environment was largely deteriorated and drab and the near-by public housing was in the form of large, colourless concrete blocks.

The plan of the individual units at Banneker is based on the traditional San Francisco flat with front and rear stairs so that the apartment groups are arranged vertically rather than horizontally along corridors. Therefore, to use strong colours in essentially vertical units seemed natural. The palette is limited to inexpensive colours readily available with a major aim being that of giving identity to particular locations but cohesiveness to the entire group.

Bay Area Rapid Transit Stations (figs. 18–20)
The BART elevated system is on a concrete structure of standard design; the standard concrete track girders run through all the overhead stations and establish the basic modular pattern and also the dominant structural characteristic. Design standards for all stations require that they be concrete. It seemed natural (particularly since the concrete was of a very high quality and a neutral off-white colour that did not interfere with one's perception of subtleties of the many colours in natural light and natural shadows) to continue the main concrete colour straight through the exterior of the station. However, the interior was another matter and light and colour were absolutely essential to give direction, to call attention to entrances and exits and to make the entire station obvious and operationally understandable to the user without either confusion or delay. While the directional and locational requirements were essentially the same for each station, a standard informational colour system was not used and the colours were varied station to station more in accordance with local environmental characteristics. Wherever possible, artists were engaged to work with the architects in the design and use of colour, but unfortunately the funds for this programme came quite late so that the ideal of having the artists participate from the start in the design was not possible.

The Colour Approach of Piano and Rogers

Richard Rogers

The Anglo-Italian practice of Piano and Rogers has, over the past decade of their individual activities and joint collaboration, developed a philosophy of problem-solving by the use of technology which incorporates a positive approach to colour in the architectural situation. The group have won many awards and competitions including first prize in the Plateau Beaubourg Arts Centre (Paris) international competition.

A strong influence on our work is the way in which colour is used as a safety factor in the coding of industrial environments and machinery: steel plants, refineries, tractors and cranes. We believe that buildings are machines, as did the modern architectural pioneers. However, our interest in the so-called 'elegant architecture' is limited, and I do not know how to handle the classical monochromatic elegance which is expressed so well in the work of Mies van der Rohe, Eero Saarinen and Philip Johnson. This has much to do with our interest in personal participation. In other words, we would like to come towards the idea that people could slip in their own red, pink or blue house-panel into a parent structure. It is another way of breaking down the scale and allowing exciting things to happen. The whole 'Miesian' thesis which states: 'you will all have special brown blinds to match the colour of my building' is contrary to our beliefs. One would like to think that one could develop a patchwork form of building which would still have the scale and possibilities of good, classical architecture.

In the Centre Beaubourg situation, the building totally exposes its works — just like an exposed watch mechanism (fig. 22). As the service systems are visible and a major part of the building, we adopted the British Standard code for industrial colours (used for marking hazards and identifying certain equipment) as a basic direction to follow; the significance being that we are seeking rules so that our colour decisions do not stem purely from arbitrary preferences. We begin colour selection, therefore, with a process of elimination through colour-coding.

A second system of elimination has been the question of impermanence. Speeded-up weathering tests have shown that certain of the brighter paint pigments, especially violets and pinks, are fugitive and are excluded for this reason. Metallic colours also tend to be excluded because they discolour and are therefore difficult to patch up later. The material we use most is steel, and, as it cannot be left unprotected, we are dealing with applied finishes such as vinyl plastic coating, especially on the ducting. The manufacturers, however, produce a limited colour range and, although we try to persuade them to manufacture other colours, they often refuse because of the added cost and this is a further form of limitation.

Our third system of elimination comes down to 'what is the building about?', especially its scale and rhythm — what Renzo Piano calls, 'the nervousness of a building'. One of the major problems of modern materials is their lack of scale. Colour, for us, is an important element in tackling this problem. Technology is advancing and we can now use more bright colours; for example, twenty years ago yellow was impossible but now, through plastic, we can achieve it just as well as any of the other primary colours.

During the Renaissance, buildings reflected the colour of natural materials or were covered in applied art. Now we can produce the applied skins — they come from the factory by the roll — one has to make a colour choice and, in turn, make a colour statement. We do not need to do this with bricks and concrete because, being naturally coloured, they weather well. Stronger environmental colours are emerging from the fact that the new materials work just as well, if not better, with pigment added to them. Why should I use black, brown or grey when plasticated steel offers such a wide range of colour? I suppose the whole thing is personalization — we have always consciously designed with colour because of our interest in what Renzo and I call 'happy buildings' — buildings that people react to.

To use Gropius's statement that all colours are beautiful is a pretty good concept, but one does have to employ some process of elimination or control, and this is partly subjective. To return to the word I find so worrying — 'elegance' — a good way of getting away from elegant detail is by using colour to underline what is important, to define elements and express our approach to architecture. The possibilities today are great and some of us are researching those possibilities in personalizing or identifying architectural space (fig. 23).

On the Use of Colour in Buildings

Foster Associates

Foster Associates are well-known for their bold use of architectural colour. A fundamental aim of the practice is to produce a truly integrated design by incorporating a range of skills into the design team from the earliest stages. Environmental engineers form an important part of the practice and are involved in decisions concerning the use of colour. Thus colour selection at Foster Associates is based on technical as well as intuitive considerations.

We have always tended to use strong colours in our buildings both internally and externally. This choice is basically an intuitive preference deriving perhaps from precedents such as the bold colours used on agricultural or contractors' machinery, or the eye-catching colours of advertisements. We enjoy the visual excitement of the juxtaposition of vivid colours and their effect on an object in the landscape.

Every problem has been approached empirically. For each building we have made bold decisions, built them at that time, and from these experiences have developed several areas of response. These have a technical calculated basis as well as being intuitive. Our scientific understanding and ability to understand and control the choice of colours has developed through the projects, as has the ability to imagine further colour combinations.

More colours are now available for the architect to use in a wider range of contexts than ever before. The range is no longer controlled by the basic colour of the material. Applied as finishes they tend to upgrade essentially low-cost roughly finished material, such as asbestos cladding, to a higher degree of finish. Developments in paints and coatings make possible finishes in any colour.

We consider colour as a tool available for use both outside and inside our buildings.

The juxtaposition of buildings in a landscape can be of two kinds: imposition of the man-made object on the landscape, or careful integration of a man-made object which is more akin to the earth — either hollowed out of it or blending in as part of the natural landscape (made of the same materials). This choice is present through history: compare, for example, a Le Corbusier white house in a green field with a Frank Lloyd Wright house of the same colour as the earth and carefully sited, or back to ancient times when a man lived in a cave at the same time as he built temples, deliberately and symbolically placed in the landscape. One is active, the other passive. In one tradition the man-made object stands almost aggressively in opposition to nature; in the other it is recessive — blending in with surroundings.

If this analogy is simplified into the two main streams of temples and caves, we could use this to categorize our own buildings. If we want to design non-dominant, 'cave-like' buildings, we tend to use glass as the main material. When used as a cladding material, the reflective properties of glass, particularly of solar-tinted or mirror glass, merge the building into the surroundings — be it the Ipswich street context of the Willis, Faber & Dumas office (fig. 40) or the wooded field reflected in the IBM office walls. These buildings reflect the colours of the surrounding environment. Our choice of colour is confined to the inside of the buildings.

On the other hand, if our response to the site is to make a more imposing statement, we tend to use vivid colour externally, to choose a deliberate counterpoint to the surroundings. The building looks as if it has been brought in: an effect reinforced by the colour. At Thamesmead, on an industrial estate, the landscape is

40
Reflections in the Willis, Faber & Dumas office building, Ipswich. Foster Associates.

scattered with a range of objects, pylons, factories, waste dumps and our blue warehouse for Modern Art Glass looks as if it recently landed amongst them (fig. 31).

The decision-making process involved in selecting colour for the internal environment depends upon our preferences and also on our increasing knowledge of the relationship between colour and light. In our early buildings the choice tended to be arbitrary. But learning from and questioning our early successes, we have achieved a greater understanding.

The warehouse for SAPA (Scandinavian Aluminium Profiles AB), for example, sits in flat, marshy Derbyshire countryside. The outside is a bland white box. In contrast inside the building all efforts were concentrated on providing sufficient visual stimulation to overcome the monotony inherent in windowless environments. The structure was painted in brilliant primary colours, the members differentiated to diagram the construction process as the colours were interpreted from the engineer's colour-coding system. The machinery used in the extrusion plants was similarly painted giving them a sculptural quality (fig. 32). These colours were selected scientifically: the internal colours give an exact response to the spectrum of the artificial lighting. Each colour in the spectrum is present in the finished building.

In the design of the internal environment of the offices for Willis, Faber & Dumas at Ipswich we went to the extent of actually building a mock-up of the finished office floor and testing the greens of the carpet, the yellow of the partitioning, under a range of tubes to ensure the right colour response. Again the colours express the diagram of the building structure: all structural elements are painted white, floor surfaces green, vertical core walls are yellow.

This building also brought us up against the complexities of colour response in natural light. This is less easily verified or tested, being changeable and not totally quantifiable. As in musical sounds where the sound spectrum is much more complex than appears on the oscilloscope, the spectrum of natural light also has almost invisible overtones which we believe still influence perception. They are not exactly definable by machine but alter the quality appreciated by the eye.

We appreciated the unquantifiable nature of the external environment most vividly in our airtent project for Computer Technology Ltd (figs. 33 and 34). There, external events, such as changing light conditions, modifying the heat response, shadows from passing birds, the noise of rain, impinged directly through the thin skin: the aspects of environmental control which can generally be ignored as the subtleties of the situation predominated.

To overcome the perception of some of these variations, a 'hot' red carpet was chosen and the link between the air structure and main building made a very warm red, though it was actually unheated.

Future decisions would seem to centre around progressing our understanding of natural light and our ability to both control it and respond to its qualities in colour choice.

64

Notes on a Colour Palette

Deborah Sussman and Paul Prejza

Whenever and wherever we travel we observe and record the environments of places with strong indigenous traditions that differ from our own. The markets of Mexico, the hilltowns of Italy, and the street life of India have been rich sources of inspiration to our work, particularly in the use of colour. Our greatest interest has been in colour used publicly in buildings, clothing, and in the market place.

We have uncovered many different cultural attitudes towards colour; the Latins tend to be freer and flamboyant with colour, Northern Europeans are more sombre and precise. But everywhere colour is used and dealt with to some degree and its use is a major factor in giving a region a character — a 'sense of place'. Observing these differences, identifying the traditions, and discovering new attitudes is a fascinating activity for anyone interested in colour.

After years of observations in many different situations and places, we are just beginning to understand a few of the complex considerations that go into creating an environment with colour.

Developing a Palette

The man (fig. 48) is painting his house. The chances are good, judging by his neighbour's experience before him, that his choice of colour will not only be compatible with the colours of his neighbours, but will actually enhance them and make the street even more exciting and still allow him his individual expression. One of the reasons this can happen is that a palette has been developed in this little Spanish town that organizes colour relationships and subconsciously controls its use. Palettes exist in most places. In Patzcuaro, Mexico, for instance, the palette is very limited — every building is painted a shade of white and a shade of terra cotta. Two hundred miles away in Guanajuato the palette is much more varied. Many different colours and intensities are used but the colours are limited to a soft, almost pastel range.

(Overleaf:)

41
The French colour palette. Samples of earth collected by Lenclos from the diverse regions of France. (photo: J. F. Godineau)

42
Lenclos's investigation essentially consists of assembling the existing architectural spectrum of an area. Here, colour plates are made from samples of building materials and natural elements collected from the site of the proposed new town at Le Vaudreuil. (photo: R. Meyer)

43
This house front situated in the old village of Le Vaudreuil is an example of the value that its occupants place on their home through individual decoration. Lenclos's colour analysis aims to objectively reproduce the rich lesson in harmonies which are to be found in traditional environments. (photo: J. F. Godineau)

44
The resulting colour synthesis of the Le Vaudreuil site including colour records of natural and man-made elements. (photo: R. Meyer)

45
The colour plates are then regrouped into colour ranges which illustrate the predominating colours of architectural elements: walls, doors, windows, etc. The above illustrates Lenclos's proposals for the wall colours of Le Vaudreuil. (photo: R. Meyer)

46
A final classification of the colours emanating from the Le Vaudreuil investigation showing proposed façade colour treatments which would permit a better integration of new and existing buildings into the site. (photo: R. Meyer)

47
Lenclos carried out a further investigation at Creteil. This is a preparatory model in a series of colour studies for apartment buildings planned for the site of the new town. The architects are Jean-Claude Bernard and Wladimir Mitrofanoff. (photo: F. Puyplat)

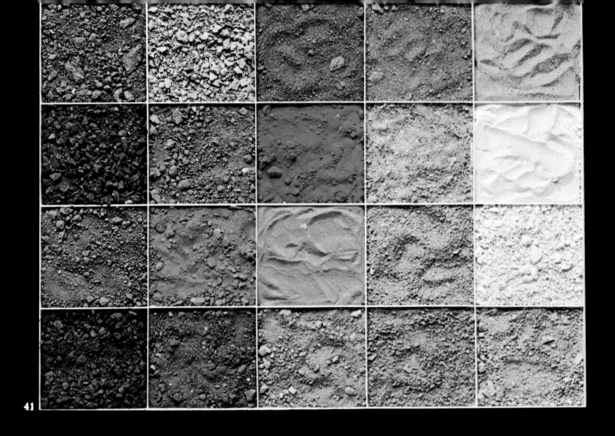

41

42

43

44

45, 46

47

48
Within a predominantly blue and pink street setting a man paints his house ochre and white in a village near Almeria, Spain.

Developing a palette is our first step in approaching a colour problem and all examples of our work illustrated here began in this manner. We designed a brochure which is probably the only example where a palette was imposed. The purpose was to showcase a new line of colour papers. Editorially, it described the work of women in the graphic arts world. The papers themselves appear to change. Unexpected relationships and the element of surprise were also used as a reminder of the contributions of women in the field. By cutting the papers at an angle and showing them in a constantly changing relationship, the palette became more active and exciting. The palette was further enriched by using different coloured inks. Being transparent, the colours of the inks took on some of the colour of the paper. For instance, a red ink had a subtle, different look when it was printed on green paper than when it was printed on pink.

In some cases, a colour palette is so strong and has been used and recognized over such a long period of time that it becomes traditional and an important part of the culture. In such instances colour becomes strongly symbolic. Towns, regions and even countries throughout history have developed a strong traditional use of colour. Siena, for instance, is an Italian town which has given its name internationally to a colour. Colours are often referred to as being Mexican, Chinese or Venetian.

This association of a colour or a colour palette with a particular place is useful in creating a mood or evoking a sense of location. In designing a centennial exhibit for a Southern Californian manufacturer of ceramics, who had a strong tie historically and in name to early Californian traditions, we developed a colour palette based on the colours found in the California missions. Our design aimed to evoke a mood of an early Californian marketplace and used several devices such as columns and furniture to help create that feeling but the colours did most to convey the mood and spirit. Seventeen paint colours were used in our palette; but they did not attempt to duplicate the colours of an actual mission. It was the mood created by them, not the specific colour itself, which combined to become an abstraction or a symbol of missions and marketplace.

Colour and Light
The effects that natural light has on colour is fascinating to observe but difficult to understand and predict. We know that shadows affect colour but have not exploited it to advantage. Colour reflection can have spectacular effects and a similar effect can be achieved more directly and predictably with transparent colours and by backlighting translucent colours. Multi-coloured transparent fringes (fig. 35) define a small open space and give it a warm rosy aura in a crowded store. Further back in the same building backlighting intensifies the colours in the graphic frieze (fig. 37) and is an effective device to pull the public to the rear of the store. We designed the colour in this way by trying to solve our client's stated need, that of circulation. We used transparent colour on an exterior canopy (fig. 39) as part of a department store that we designed. During the day sunlight streams through the multi-coloured panels and the colour is transmitted to the sidewalk and the passer-by below. At night the tiny lights inside the canopy make the colours glow. The canopy makes reference to its surrounding area, filled with ornate movie theatres and to the Latin shoppers in that part of Los Angeles.

The Mexicans recognize the value of coloured light and use it extensively. The sign illustrated (fig. 38) is an elaborate example. An American sign (fig. 36) incorporating our symbol for Standard Shoes is in the same spirit, and is made of different colours of neon tubing. Both signs are effective during the daytime as well as at night.

Using Colour
Unfortunately, no simple formula for using colour exists. Work done in analysing, codifying and developing colour systems has been useful but provides no sure success for an exciting and harmonious use of colour in the environment. To begin to understand how colour is used and colour traditions develop, we go back to the man painting his house. To paraphrase Ed Bacon in the *Design of Cities,* this man, like his neighbours, had, 'thousands of times since childhood, experienced the colours and colour relationships in his town. Because of the size and scale of his town, his apprehension of it and its colours is complete and simultaneous. All parts of it and all its details are at one instant a part of his mental equipment. As he decided what colour to paint his house it naturally and inevitably fitted in with forms and colours surrounding him.

(Overleaf:)

49
Crane at the Acièrie Solmer steel complex at Fos-sur-mer near Marseilles. In an attempt to humanize the giant mechanical form Lenclos in the Urbame team uses rich colour on each of its components as a means of breaking down the scale. (photo: J.-Ph. Lenclos)

50
Shigeta's use of colour at the Dainichi Seika chemical factory in Japan. (photo: T. Sukahara)

51
Lenclos's colour proposal for the cement works at Mantes near Paris. (photo: J.-Ph. Lenclos)

52
The initial stages of Lenclos's colour analysis with the Urbame team for the integration of a dockyard complex into the surrounding harbour town of La Ciotat near Marseilles. (photo: J.-Ph. Lenclos)

53
Lenclos's colour prescription for the AGA factory in the industrial zone of Limay Porcheville. (photo: J.-Ph. Lenclos)

50 51

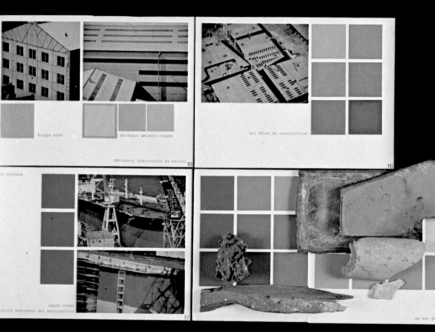

52

53

'This phenomenon, often referred to as "intuitive", actually represents a process so complex that no computer yet conceived can come close to duplicating it.'

Our work with colours also utilizes an 'intuitive' approach. Literally hundreds of different colours are examined, chosen, studied, eliminated, and added to, just to find the right grouping or palette. This grouping may consist of six, twelve, or thirty colours, and include paints, laminates, dyes, fabrics, inks, papers, and building materials. Some of the colours reviewed may never be used, but in some cases they are all used.

This method of working with colour was developed while working over an extended period of time with Ray Eames. Her disciplined, organic approach offered a method for seeing, selecting, and using colour that is invaluable.

Only by constantly working with and observing colour in the environment can we begin to develop the kind of facility with it that seems so natural to the Spanish man painting his house.

Living in Colour

Jean-Philippe Lenclos

In 1965 Jean-Philippe Lenclos became the art director of the Société des Peintures Gauthier, a French company producing heavy-duty paint. He gave it a company image, designed its trademark, its graphics and packaging, as well as its colour charts. From this experience with product design, Lenclos then directed his colour expertise towards architecture in France, where there is an extreme diversity of climates, from Mediterranean to Nordic, and a corresponding variety of building materials adapted to the local weather conditions. His method of investigation is both simple and objective and he now records his process of analysis which attempts to codify the language of environmental colour.

The Analysis

The subject of architectural colour in the modern landscape is essentially concerned with the visual quality of architecture, whether the environment be natural, urban, or industrial. The environment is our collective domain; any change in it concerns us all and cannot be left to the whim or fancy of arbitrary choice or of sweeping decisions, whatever the motive. It is high time we became involved in this vital problem if we are to protect those areas which have not yet been too badly spoiled.

In order to arrive at a better chromatic conception of modern construction and standardized materials in the building industry, it seemed essential to carry out a methodical analysis of the colours which are characteristic of each of the French regions. This analysis, conducted on behalf of the Société des Peintures Gauthier and begun in 1967, led me to develop an original method of approach which was based on an objective observation of the phenomenon of colour in architecture.

The first phase of this study enabled me to establish a synthesis of chromatic components characteristic of the architecture of each region which clearly illustrated their respective differences. The results enabled me to create, as a guide to the painting of buildings, a full range of paints matching the predominating colours of each region. A user's guide, called *Selecteur d'Harmonies,* initially summed up the first phase of my research and it presented plates of related colour combinations intended for the façades of buildings. Apart from suggesting a practical system of colour selection for decorators, the *Selecteur d'Harmonies* can also serve as a practical guide for industrial designers and colour practitioners such as architects, whether they plan to use colour to identify or contrast with the existing environment.

My regional analysis aims to identify the predominating characteristics and chromatic detail of the existing architecture in a given area, both in general and in detailed form. In order to select subjects for analysis, individual houses or groups of buildings are chosen as being representative, i.e., embodying typical architectural and colour qualities in keeping with their environment.

(1) Architecture in relation to its mineral and vegetable environment – the analysis of the basic colours of a region

One has only to collect a little soil from each of the French regions in order to discover the amazing range of natural colours (fig. 41). In the past, towns developed in a period of limited transportation and, logically, were constructed from local materials: earth from the quarry and sand from the river were the most common components of traditional French construction. Their mortar, daub, plaster and colour wash are the visual translation of the pigment of local sand and clay, which establishes a close link between the earth and the dwelling.

Progressively built-up in this accumulative fashion town façades take on an individual chromatic quality. This is illustrated by the granite of Brittany, micaceous chalk found in Touraine and the bricks of the North. In Picardy there is a striking comparison between the walls of St Quentin and Soissons. St. Quentin is a very colourful town, mainly built of brick which is sharply contrasted by the rich colours of its doors and shutters. Soissons, situated only fifty kilometres away, is built of ashlar masonry, and its appearance is almost monochromatic. The palette of chalky colour at Soissons, fading on walls and shutters, is matched in sobriety by the subtle shades of its grey roofscape.

The geographical setting and climatic conditions generate a diversity of roofscapes which vary considerably from one region to another. Indigenous materials used in roof construction strongly influence the formal appearance of a town, particularly when its location offers an over-all view of its structure. The shape and slope of roof forms can radically alter the proportion of the coloured elements. However, it is interesting to note that, in general, the total palette of a French town never exceeds more than two or three basic hues.

Beyond the objective study of minerals, soil, building materials and paint, we turn to the more subjective aspect of our study: the random factors and elements which are subject to changing colour — light, sky, water and vegetation.

Although a building may reflect the same range of colour as its mineral environment, its colour is not static. It evolves, shifts and changes seasonally as a result of changes in light, air, humidity, rain and drought. In addition, natural parasites, such as mosses and lichens, add to the charm of the materials in the passage of time.

(2) Qualitative and quantitative relationships of colour in the various architectural elements – the analysis of the precise colours of a building
This investigation essentially consists of assembling the existing architectural spectrum of an area or site based on a systematic evaluation of the component elements and materials of a building.

Phase One: The Methodical Examination of the Sites
Our method at this initial stage of the study is to rely, as far as possible, on the objective evidence provided by the architecture and its environment. Basically, this involves taking samples directly from the selected areas. We methodically collect samples of materials and paint from the earth, walls, roofs, doors, shutters, etc., together with other natural substances such as moss and lichen. If a sample is impossible to obtain, a painted colour match is made on the spot (figs. 42 and 43).

Phase Two: The Synthesis of Collected Data
A long and meticulous process of synthesis now begins in the studio. All the collected samples are examined and translated into painted colour plates which faithfully reproduce the original colours. The colour plates are then classified and re-grouped into panels which produce a colour synthesis of both a region and of its architectural elements (figs. 44 and 45).

Phase Three: A system of Chromatic Conceptualization
The result of our field study and studio synthesis is the presentation of an applied colour vocabulary appropriate to each of the regions of France. Two colour programmes are evolved which are co-ordinated so that they can combine to offer harmony and variety in their application to existing or proposed future building projects (figs. 46 and 47).

The same method was employed by Lenclos in a colour study for Tokyo, carried out in collaboration with the Japanese Colour Planning Centre in 1970. For this analysis, he divided the city into four main areas: the traditional buildings of the old city; the modern buildings in the new districts; mixed or transitional areas; and the industrial zone. This division demonstrates Lenclos's acknowledgement that, in general, buildings are no longer surrounded by natural landscape but by other buildings. In these cases, just as in traditional situations, Lenclos believes that the role of colour is a vital aid to architectural intent and should be seriously considered at the outset of any urban design programme.

Colour in the Modern and Industrial Landscape

Present-day architecture no longer responds sympathetically to the natural landscape but, by its breadth and scale, creates its own landscape and its own environment. Industrially produced materials are progressively becoming less connected to the site; synthetic materials of every kind and origin are distributed and indifferently employed anywhere with an ever-growing risk of neutralizing what was once the original and essential visual quality of the architecture in different regions and countries.

Colour in modern architecture can, therefore, be conceived in new terms: the simultaneous construction of large-scale complexes which, being out of context with nature, create new urban landscapes. Two specific kinds of landscape emerge: the urban complex (housing, etc.) and the industrial zones.

The dimensions of the modern town or city, particularly where there are high-rise buildings, make it difficult to introduce the natural elements which act as an important link with, and symbol of, living nature. Certainly, colour is no remedy for this irreplaceable link but by its plastic and rhythmical powers of expression it is able to release a poetic dimension which complements the man-made environment. Here, colour in material, structure, rhythm, contrast, can be a new plastic language whose riches are offered to the city of tomorrow. The recent intervention of the 'colour concept', considered as a completely separate entity from planning and architecture, reveals two divergent schools of thought: on the one hand, pictorial and expressive polychromy which breaks with tradition and, on the other, the search for an integrated polychromy — not expressly imitative as regards the site and tradition but arising from a creative process which takes these two factors into consideration.

Today, one can see some experiments which take us towards the idea of a coloured city. Supergraphics are one of the significant manifestations of this new development. Even if this vocabulary as well as its existence in the architectural setting is new, one could say that supergraphics have existed throughout time. Nature, which provides a universal reference source, offers the best examples. Underwater fauna are full of such examples such as the exotic fish with their bold stripes, but consider too the cows in the meadows with their random dappling. Without our really being aware of it supergraphics are all around us; shadows which, according to the laws of projection and the shape of objects which interrupt the light source, fall across every plane — the shadows of foliage, the gigantic shadows of clouds which trace a moving supergraphic design over the countryside. Since antiquity, man has employed supergraphics in ritual make-up which transforms the human body and intensifies the facial form in order to project a different image. The make-up of the Chinese theatre or of the Japanese Kabuki offer countless examples of supergraphics which precede its use in architecture (figs. 54–7).

Supergraphics, whether applied to mobile or static objects, is a graphic art which is applied to a volumetric surface without submitting to its contours. It covers planes, edges and corners enhancing the initial scale of the mass. By the power of its pattern,

54
Supergraphics — fish.

55
Supergraphics — cow.

56
Supergraphics — clouds.

57
Supergraphics — Japanese Kabuki.

to which is added the expressive strength of contrast and colour, it plays a real part in creating considerable visual transformations of architectural space.

Environmental colour is one of the visual elements which link and act as a common denominator operating on all levels and in each discipline. An interaction between complementary disciplines is equally valid when it is a question of conceiving and building entire cities as it is in smaller entities whether public or private which are, when programmed as a whole, just as complex. At the conceptual and analytical stage it is necessary to put aside that irrational and subjective approach to which colour was formerly reduced. Indeed, colour may no longer here be considered solely as an intuitive language limited to the function of creating atmosphere or considered as a matter of taste. It is a necessary element in the fulfilment of a wide concept in which all aspects are considered to enhance its objective role in the service of safety, hygiene, information or marketing.

Today, architectural colour is an important element in the treatment of the industrial area in which an essentially technical and functional architecture helps to assert the artificial character of the environment. In both the context of new industrial zones and the older, more isolated factories which, when expanded, threaten to spoil the original quality of a site, it is now realized that the role played by colour extends far beyond the more aesthetic function which has been previously attributed to it.

Perhaps the most important function of colour is to 'humanize' an all too often bold and austere architecture or to simply create a more congenial work environment. However, it would be useless to attribute too much psychological power to colour as happened when the Functional Colour movement appeared in the 1950s. This attractive label seduced businessmen who were concerned either with profit margins or with the well-being of their personnel.

In my opinion, architectural colour is a relational, developmental system which is clearly linked to the specific character of each design programme. Particularly, industrial buildings are a natural subject for a positive chromatic statement for industrial zones often occupy vast areas of space and are removed from the traditional context. For example, the immense Solmer iron and steel complex at Fos-sur-mer enabled the Urbame team (with whom I had to work out the planning problems) to define and execute a clear and efficient coding system in which the buildings themselves provided the basis for colour application. Each industrial unit had a clearly defined perimeter which was identified by the use of a range of predominating colours (fig. 49). Situated several kilometres away from each other, these units could therefore be identified at a distance and the general plan more easily recognized by the workers.

Apart from its architectural quality, colour can also be used as a means of visual identity in the promotion of a company image. When defined clearly, colour can transform architecture into a visual advertisement. A masterly example of this is the Japanese chemical pigment factory where the painter, Shigeta, transformed the chimneys into extraordinary vertical objects of rhythm and colour (fig. 50).

A new generation of architects is discovering colour as a further dimension in the creation and expression of architecture. They are 'men of art' who combine the qualities of painter, *coloriste,* form-giver, and designer who take us towards the idea of the polychrome city.

4   A Definition of Colour for the Designer

Although we take our perception of colour for granted, a very complex mechanism of vision makes it possible. The system is still insufficiently understood and there exists as yet no simple scientific theory to account for it. We do know, however, certain basic facts which are the result of years of scientific investigation among physicists, chemists, physiologists and psychologists.

Colour is a subjective sensation caused by light and is not properly a quality which is inherent in the object itself. Because we are used to living in daylight and other light conditions where one has a reasonably continuous spectrum in the illumination, we learn to associate colours with particular objects, such as grass or an orange, and subsequently project back from our mind the colour that we normally associate with that object. For example, a green table is not inherently green, although it may appear to be that colour in daylight conditions. It can, in fact, appear as quite different colours when viewed under different light sources such as mercury or sodium vapour.

In general terms colour does not exist without light, because colour is a sensation conveyed through the medium of energy in the form of light radiations within the visible spectrum. Without an observer these rays do not, in themselves, constitute colour. As Sir Isaac Newton explained in his *Optiks,* 'The rays are not coloured. In them there is nothing else than a power to stir up a sensation of this or that colour'. It is the eye and brain of the observer which interpret the meaning of these energy messages and perceive them as a sensation of colour.

The perception of colour depends upon four important factors and our graphic representation (fig. 58) offers a conceptual model from which we can discuss some of the most important contributions from the highly specialized and diverse fields of scientific inquiry.

(1) The spectral energy distribution of the *light* (the conditions under which the colour is being perceived).

(2) The spectral characteristics of the *object,* in respect to absorption, reflection, transmission.

(3) The sensitivity of the *eye* and *brain.*

78

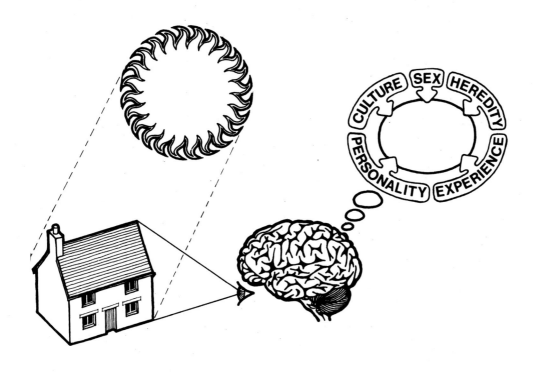

58

(4) The *psychological factors* (the experience and personality of the viewer). As physiological, psychological and physical qualities are all involved they will be dealt with in turn.

(1) Light

No object appears coloured at low levels of illumination, such as moonlight. There is a threshold of illumination below which colour cannot be seen. While the light level can be enough for perception of shape, movement and the size of objects, there has to be a higher level of illumination before colour is seen. This can be demonstrated if we imagine a red sign painted on a white building. As night turns into day we would be able still to read the sign's letters in very low levels of illumination, but the daylight has to increase quite considerably before the sign is perceived as red.

Correct colour rendering requires the right kind of light — light which contains a full spectrum without any excessive dominance of energy at any wavelength. Here we must return to the example of the green table: if we were to subject it to coloured lights (red, blue and yellow) it would be seen that the table is no longer green. Although light has been projected on to it, it has not been the 'right type of light' containing a full spectrum.

In more technical terms light is simply the name given to one narrow region of energy that is constantly radiating from the sun. Newton, by placing a prism in front of a beam of sunlight, observed a band of ordered colours which he called 'spectrum' (Latin for 'sight'). The colours of the spectrum vary in wavelength: the distance between the crest of one energy wave and the next and the visible range of wavelengths runs from 400 to 750 nanometres (a billionth of a metre).

Newton's original experiment led to the first and most celebrated theory of colour perception. Using a second inverted prism, he demonstrated that if all the colours of the spectrum are recombined, white light is obtained. However, his most striking experiment was when, by mixing red, green and blue beams of light, he also obtained white light. The fact that white light results from a mixture of these three colours makes it possible for the other colours of the spectrum to be obtained by mixing these three hues in different proportions (in fact we can produce some colours such as purple which are not in the spectrum). This was the basis of the theory proposed by Thomas Young and later developed by H. von Helmholtz who have suggested that there are three kinds of light receptors in the human eye corresponding to the wavelengths of red, green and blue and that all the other colours are the result of combining those three; yellow, for example, is the result of a red–green combination

Different energy distributions of various light sources (artificial suns)
The light from a tungsten filament lamp has a very low energy at the blue end of the spectrum (400 nm) and a relatively high energy at the red end (700 nm). A light source of this type has a dominantly orange-red energy and its colour-rendering property would be to emphasize the orange-redness of an object, and minimize the blue-greenness. (How many designers have painted artwork under this type of common light source and been shocked at the intensity of the blues and greens when viewed in daylight?)

In the case of fluorescent tubes (gas discharge lamps) the bulk of radiant energy is contained within very narrow spectral bandwidths and, although the lamp can be made to emit energy throughout the spectrum by the use of fluorescent phosphors, the dominant energy is always in the mercury lines and, therefore, the colour rendering of these lights is not 'normal'. A 'black body', such as the interior of a furnace, can be heated to different temperatures and at a certain temperature it starts to emit visible radiations. It becomes 'red hot' at this temperature and is emitting a high proportion of the red part of the spectrum and very little of the blue. As the heat is increased, so the amount of light emitted increases through yellow to white heat and the spectral distribution changes the relative proportion of the blue end of the spectrum, increasing all the time. Thus sunlight can be expressed in terms of 'colour temperature', and this is a convenient method of specifying the energy distribution of a light source.

The spectral energy distribution of all the common light sources such as daylight, tungsten filament lamps, fluorescent tubes and sodium street lighting varies considerably so that when dealing with colour — particularly in its design aspects — we have to consider which will be the best and most appropriate type of light to use: in a self-service restaurant it is important to make the food appear appetizing and good to eat. The colour of meat, bacon, pies, sausages and other meat foods is enhanced by the orange–red light energy of tungsten light, whereas they would appear duller, greyer if displayed in the light from a fluorescent tube. Fluorescent tubes giving a warmer, redder light could be chosen or, better still, perhaps a mixture of the two types of illumination.

In shops selling face powders, lipsticks, eyeshadow and other coloured cosmetics which may be worn in daylight or various types of artificial light, it is important that the colour intended is the colour clearly seen. An eyeshadow material which can be pleasantly blue in daylight could very easily appear grey in tungsten filament light and this would not enhance the beauty of the eye of the wearer — it would, or could, look like a black eye!

The Dimensions of Colour
Thus far we have discussed colour in terms of the spectral *hues* and as various kinds

of light source. In the world of colour, however, we can discriminate between 300,000 tints and shades through differences due to the purity and brightness of colours. If, for example, we add grey to a red the chromatic strength or value of that desaturated red is weakened; in fact if we add any other colour to our red, the purity, chromatic strength — sometimes called *saturation* — of that red will diminish. Black, grey and white are sometimes referred to as achromatic colours as they lack both hue and saturation. The third and different way in which we can distinguish colours is in terms of their *brightness,* which roughly corresponds to the amount of physical energy or intensity of the light.

The process of mixing patches of coloured light as in Newton's experiments is sometimes called *additive colour mixture* as distinct from the subtractive colour mixture which occurs when we mix coloured pigments such as in printing or painting. Another way of mixing colour additively is by spinning a colour wheel fast enough so that the colours visually 'fuse'. Certain hues when mixed in this way, such as blue and yellow, will produce grey; these colours are called *complementary* and in the same way one can find a complement for each colour.

Psychologists have attempted to explain our visual perception of colour in simple graphic models. Most of these representations have deliberately ignored the physical composition in terms of wavelength as they have concentrated on the psychological perception of colour. Several diagrams, shapes and solids have been produced from these attempts and figure 59 is a classic example showing Newton's spectrum bent into a colour circle. The hues along the periphery of the colour circle represent the various colours of the spectrum with complementary colours appearing approximately opposite to each other. The second colour dimension —

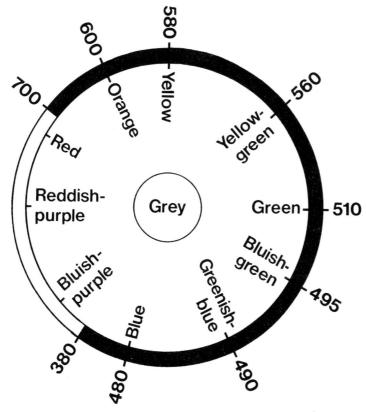

59
The colour circle, showing the principle hues and their positions around its perimeter. The numbers, in nanometres, indicate the wavelengths of light corresponding to the hues.

saturation — is represented by the distance of each fully saturated colour at the periphery of the circle from the achromatic grey of the centre. The third colour dimension can be visualized as a vertical axis representing brightness, dazzle and white at the top, and black or darkness at the bottom. In this way the three colour dimensions of hue, saturation and brightness have been turned into three-dimensional colour cones or solids.

Attempts to classify or specify colour by dividing, scaling and numbering each of these three dimensions resulted in several systems of colour notation. Of the earlier attempts, possibly the Ostwald and Munsell systems are the best known.

(2) Object

The world we live in is a spatial one; we convert information from our environment from two-dimensional retinal images into three-dimensional information — our brains seem to 'reconstruct' space by taking into consideration distance and depth. Space without content, however, is meaningless; space is defined by objects which act as visual agents which have perceptual properties of their own such as size, shape, texture and colour.

In a strict sense, objects have no intrinsic colour because we can only see them if they reflect light. They have no energy of their own to reflect and you may recall our examples of how different types of illumination directly affect the colour of objects (although we do take into consideration changes in natural and artificial illumination during a day and the seasonal cycles and compensate for these changes through what psychologists call 'colour constancy' by which objects seem to retain their colour despite changes in lighting). However, if we take light for granted, we can consider colour as a property of objects in so far as it is the physical and chemical composition of the objects which will determine how much light is to be absorbed and how much to be reflected.

Most of the colour which we see in our daily lives is formed subtractively. A red object appears red because it has the property of absorbing (subtracting) from the white light everything except the red component of the light. A pigment has the quality of absorbing some parts of the white light and the colour which the eye sees results from the remainder of the light which is left. A red table in sunlight will absorb all the wavelengths except those of the 650 nm region of the spectrum which are reflected to our eyes — hence our perception of a 'red' table. A white table will reflect all wavelengths and, as all wavelengths mixed together produce white, we see white. A black table, on the other hand, will absorb all wavelengths and appear black.

(3) The Eye and Brain

The third component of our conceptual model of colour perception is the operation of the eye and brain. No detailed anatomical or physiological description is necessary to understand their importance in seeing. On the other hand, a distinction is made between the relative importance of these two organs as some research is concentrated on the eye and some on the brain.

The sensory message reaching our eyes is not a colour experience until it reaches the brain. The idea that colour is 'seen' in our brain is, therefore, correct in this sense. A blind man, who regains his sight and sees for the first time, has then to learn which colour is red, blue or green. We can experience colour in our dreams and it can even be consciously induced with our eyes closed through pressure on the eyeball. Colour responses can also be elicited from black and white patterns such as Op Art pictures or the rotation of Benham's top — a black and white patterned wheel which, when spun, produces sensations of colour. These colour sensations are experienced entirely in the brain and exist without light or the need for a coloured object.

Light-sensitive nerve cells, known as *rods,* are located in the retina at the back of the eye. These are closely packed over the back of the retina but more widely spaced in the central field of vision. The rods are sensitive to light and not to colour, having no selective sensitivity to red, yellow, green or blue. They only give perception of white, grey and black. They are sensitive to very low levels of light and virtually go out of action at high levels of illumination. The rods enable us to see a lighted match at about one and a half miles distance and to further demonstrate their sensitivity it has been said that, given a clear night, it would take the glow from only ten strategically sited bonfires to relay a signal from Land's End in England to John O' Groats in Scotland.

There are also colour receptors in the eye known as *cones,* and these are also located in the retina, especially closely packed in a small rod-free area known as the *fovea.* This is an area of about one square millimetre and contains in the region of fifty thousand cones, although there are seven million distributed across the retina.

The only place in the retina which has no rods or cones is called the 'blind spot'. It is at this very point where the optic nerve sends messages to the visual projection area of the brain. From there, neural activity spreads to other parts of the brain such as the 'visual association region'.

As the colour receptors (cones) are very tightly packed in the *fovea* it means that our best colour discrimination is limited to a narrow field in the centre of vision, and at wider angles our critical judgement of colour declines as more and more rods are brought into action. Therefore, the quality of perceived colour depends upon its position in the visual field. If we stare at a point in front of us, a coloured object entering our vision from the side would progressively change as it approached our fixation point. At the edge of our visual field, the object would appear grey. Then, as it moved across, its blueness followed by its yellowness would become apparent. Its red and green characteristics would appear only when the object approaches the centre of our field of vision. As can be seen from the diagram (fig. 60), the area of the complementary colours of blue and yellow is much larger than the respective area of red and green. Christine Ladd-Franklin's evolutionary theory of colour vision springs from this very point. She suggests that originally the primitive eye was entirely made up of rods which perceived only a grey world. Then, as the eye evolved, the rods split into the blue-yellow sensitive cones and, finally, the yellow sensitive cones subdivided into the red and green receptors.

The Ladd-Franklin evolutionary theory also relates to colour blindness which, resulting from one or more sets of receptors being partly weak or completely out of action, is basically an hereditary characteristic and cannot be changed. This theory, therefore, appeals to the incidence of anomalous colour vision in that total colour blindness is very rare indeed; this is followed by the yellow-blue colour blindness of less than 1 per cent of the population and, finally, to the most common colour defect of red-green deficiency which coincides with the central colours in the indirect vision experiments. As this theory, however, makes assumptions especially on evolutionary grounds, it is the least accepted and is in need of more concrete facts in order to be substantiated. On the other hand, the Young-Helmholtz trichromatic theory of colour vision based on the three primaries of red–green–blue explains colour mixture but does not account for the unitary appearance of yellow.

If we return to the colour cone as a model which represents the perceived colour experience rather than the physical energy of the spectrum, there are further psychological colour experiences which require explanation. For example, we have

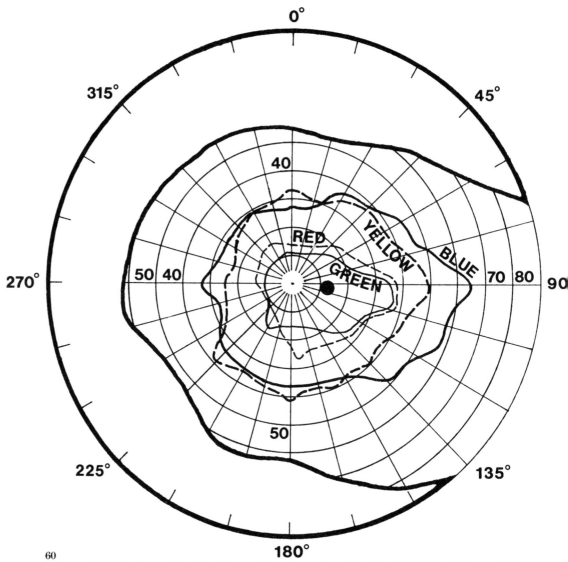

Colours visible in indirect vision. The diagram shows the portion of the visual field of the right eye within which each of the colours can be seen when the stimulus is a small patch of homogeneous light.

noted that the admixture of two diametrically opposed hues in the colour circle, such as yellow and blue, will produce grey and that each colour in the circle similarly has its complementary. The reader may have also experienced an after-image illusion. A *negative* after-image is experienced by staring at a coloured object for approximately half a minute and then directing our gaze elsewhere. The complementary colour of the object is then 'seen'. The same negative after-image can be experienced from black and white objects and a common example is the 'lingering' image on a television screen perceived after the set has been switched off. Not all after-images are negative, however, and a *positive* after-image — which is the same hue as the original sensation — is sometimes seen after a short exposure to a very bright colour.

A further example of our psychological experience of colour is *adaptation*. By staring continuously at a colour such as yellow, a change in the colour takes place. The yellow gradually appears greyer. This process of adaptation is similar to the way our eyes adjust to a darkened room after being exposed to strong sunlight, and again readjust to the yellowness of artificial illumination when we switch on the light.

84

Contrast is yet another way in which the appearance of colours can vary. In general there is a tendency for our visual system to accentuate differences between colours related either in space or in time. This phenomenon is called *simultaneous colour contrast* (spatial) or *successive colour contrast* (temporal). Simultaneous contrast, in short, is the effect on all observers that one colour has on another when they are viewed together.

This characteristic is important in graphic reproduction, interior design, art, printing and textile design and is a subjective characteristic common to all observers. This psychological experience of colour interaction is, as in the case of negative after-images, affected by the complementary nature of all colours and relates back to the colour-pair zones identified in the indirect vision experiments.

The evidence from our psychological experience of colour phenomena together with the colours seen in indirect vision indicates that we are not dealing with three primary colours but with pairs of double-acting colour receptors and processes. If, for example, in the case of negative after-images, a blue stimulus is removed from the field of vision the blue process stops and the opposite process begins — resulting in a yellow 'perception'. These points were, in fact, taken as the basis of Ewald Hering's theory proposed in 1872 and known as the Hering Opponent-Colour theory. Hering's theory postulates that there are three pairs of processes, each consisting of two opponent or opposite colours (red-green, blue-yellow and white-black). As the colour members of each pair are opponents, we cannot experience them simultaneously as, for example, we cannot say that we perceive a reddish green or a bluish yellow. If both members of the pair are equally stimulated, they cancel each other out and we see grey. L. M. Hurvich and D. Jameson proposed a modern version of this theory in the late 1950s which offers a quantitative and mathematical explanation for most of the facts of colour vision such as colour mixture, colour blindness and colour phenomena.

In some of the most recent neurophysiological work, support is given to both the Young-Helmholtz Trichromatic and Hering Opponent theories at the two different levels of the eye and brain. W. A. H. Rushton, in 1962, developed a technique in England for measuring cone pigments in the human eye by measuring the light which is reflected from the back of the retina; the quality of this reflected light was affected by any visual pigment that it passed through. In these experiments he discovered three different types of cone pigments corresponding to green, red and blue lights. This brilliant experiment was followed by some formidable work carried out by Edward F. MacNichol Jr in the United States using an instrument called a microspectrophotometer in which the absorption of light in single cones can be studied. By passing monochromatic light through the photopigment contained in a cone, he measured the amount of light absorbed by the pigment at different wavelengths. His results support Rushton's work as he found three cone pigments responding to red, green and blue lights.

These important experiments offer strong support to the Young-Helmholtz Trichromatic theory at the retinal level. However, further electrophysiological experiments behind the retina, along the optic nerve, and in the higher nervous system of the brain, indicate that there are nerve cells responding to colour in a manner consistent with Hering's Opponent-Colour theory; i.e., there are brain cells (neurons) responding in an 'on-off' fashion to either blue and yellow or red and green. The Swedish psychologist, G. Svaetichin, discovered two opponent pairs of colour — precisely those suggested by Hering: red–green and yellow–blue. By stimulating a single neuron with a red light he found that it responded in one direction and that the same neuron, when subjected to a green light, responded in the opposite direction. This same neuron, however, did not respond to any other colour. In the same way, he found that another neuron responded in the 'on-off' fashion to blue and yellow light.

The American neurologist, R. L. De Valois, has also shown that there are neurons in the brains of monkeys which 'fire' when red light is shone on the retina but are inhibited by green light.

This then is the present limit of scientific attempts to understand how we perceive colour. The Young-Helmholtz theory offers an understanding of the visual processing of colour by the eye and the Hering theory appears to be the most satisfactory explanation of our final perception of colour in the brain. It accounts for most of the colour phenomena discussed thus far. For this reason we present later in chapter six an explanation of the Natural Colour System based on Hering's theory, devised by Sven Hesselgren and developed by Anders Hård of the Swedish Colour Centre. It is a further basis for the designer to understand and communicate the colour experience.

(4) Psychological Factors

The final part of our conceptual model is the most intricate of the colour perception process.

Thus far, we have looked at the components which make colour vision possible, and also at their relative importance in our 'seeing' model. As far as the scientific knowledge goes, the designer could understand how much is known and put this into perspective with his own design philosophy. He could manipulate the physical composition of wavelength to produce various colour effects. In understanding the phenomenon of after-images, he could ensure whether they occur or not through the selection of appropriate colour relationships. He could directly apply the principles of colour contrast and assimilation to produce the maximum effects in the appearance of his buildings. In these ways the designer can begin to determine the physical appearance of the built environment and, to an extent, the way in which we perceive it.

This part of our model is of fundamental importance to the designer who wishes to invoke a particular mood or atmosphere through the use of colour. How does colour affect the observer? Is it the hue dimension of colour which affects us or the degree of brightness or saturation of that colour? How conclusively and in what circumstances would the same colours induce the same response?

However, with our receptors being daily bombarded with a plethora of stimulation, what is finally perceived will depend upon our experience, personality and interests. For example, we might be highly fashion conscious or completely unaware of the colour of the shirt we wear. Also, our psychological and genetic predisposition will influence our perception of colour. Are we, therefore, more likely to overact to certain colours because we may be more nervous and extraverted than stable and introverted?

The final destination of the visual messages after they are relayed from the back of the brain to the 'visual association region' and beyond is a complex affair which neurophysiologists have not yet resolved. We do know, however, that what is experienced, learned and associated with different colours comes into contact and interplay with our genetic predisposition. Whether our ultimate response is due to the physical energy of the colour itself or to its associations and symbolic meaning is yet another question involving the nature-nurture controversy.

As these psychological factors are of basic importance to the way we emotionally respond to colour, they will be dealt with in more detail and included in the presentation of colour research and architectural psychology papers which follow.

5 Test Findings, Observations and Notes on the Effects of Colour

(1) Studies on the Psycho-Physiological Effects of Light and Colour

'A psychologist, hired from Cambridge, had planned the decorations — magenta and gamboge; colours which — it had been demonstrated by experiments on poultry and mice — conduce to a mood of dignified gaiety.' Evelyn Waugh *Scoop*

There has always been much speculation concerning the psychological and physiological effects of colours. As a result of this general interest, our response to coloured stimuli became one of the first areas of serious psychological investigation towards the end of the nineteenth century. This was made possible with the advent of a more refined experimental technique, but the early studies were hampered by a limited knowledge of experimental method and inadequate means of measuring both the coloured stimulus and the responses to it. It is only during the last few years that any real progress has been made with the recording of some essentially basic responses, following the development of more sophisticated techniques of analysis.

The healing power of colour has been realized and practised for many centuries in the East, where a 'colour cure' has been used not only for psychological disorders but also for physical ailments. In India, for example, coloured light was projected on to ailing patients — specific colours being seen as remedial for particular symptoms and stages of disease. The study of the potentially therapeutic effect of colour in the West has been mainly limited to hospital patients suffering from psychological disorders or brain damage. It has indicated that our response to colour is total, affecting our emotions and the whole of our organism. The investigations of K. Goldstein (1942), R. Gerrard (1958) and A. Metzger, suggest a basic pattern of response in human subjects. They indicate that different colours elicit different responses related to both subjective feelings and objective physical behaviour. Responses have also been detected in insects, birds, fish and animals. Coloured light even physically affects colour-blind animals and both blind and blindfolded human beings.

The biological effect of colour has been described in many articles and papers published by Faber Birren. In these, he cites investigations which have noted the profound influence of coloured light over living organisms. He describes an experiment where ants were placed in a space illuminated by a complete spectrum.

They moved away from the ultra-violet region and took refuge in the red. Conversely, a similar test with beetles and mosquitoes observed that they were more attracted to blue and ultra-violet light than to red.

The tests reported here were carried out using coloured light as opposed to surface pigment, not only because of the greater ease with which colours can be changed but also because, with light, a far greater immersion of colour can be achieved. Both the empirical evidence and that of the controlled scientific investigation into the psycho-physiological responses support Gerrard's conclusion that 'the response to colour is differential, that it is lawful and predictable'. Our responses seem to be primarily a function of the wavelength composition and intensity of the colour stimulus, but are also mediated by other factors such as past learning, experience and personality variables.

One of the most dynamic aspects of coloured illumination is how it can be used to modify the colour, pattern, and form of architectural components and the spaces they define. This means that the visual characteristics of a given environment can be transformed without changing its physical structure or existing colour simply by changing the colour of the illumination within it.

Coloured Illumination and the Environment

Prof. Robert Preusser

Although coloured artificial lighting has been exploited in outdoor advertising, theatrical production, expositions, bars, discotheques, etc., its potential for enhancing an expanded range of man-made environments has yet to be explored. This neglect has been largely due to illumination engineering practice primarily concerned with achieving ever-increasing quantities of light rather than capitalizing upon its qualitative attributes. Coloured light sources are quantitatively inefficient. The more saturated the colour, the less lumen output per watt input and the lower the lighting level measured in footcandles.

Despite evidence to the contrary, the lighting industry has perpetuated the myth that low lighting levels and contrasting brightness are harmful to the eye. Ignoring the phenomenal adaptive power of the eye and the need for exercise to retain its elasticity, evenly distributed high lighting levels (necessary only for the most critical seeing tasks) have become standard in most architectural spaces regardless of the activities for which they are designed.

A long-held theory that the degree of efficiency in performing visual tasks is in direct ratio to the amount of footcandles provided and the assumption that visual comfort is synonymous with visual acuity has led to a doubling of recommended light levels approximately every decade for more than half a century.

In seeking solutions to the energy crisis recent studies in the U.S.A. indicate that three to ten footcandles provide sufficient light for reading and that an excess of that amount can be tiring to the eye. However, sixty to seventy footcandles are now common practice in American schools, libraries, and offices. The glare of excessive brightness and the monotony of wall to wall luminous ceilings have been the consequences of a grossly exaggerated need for more and more light.

The necessity to conserve on energy will inevitably reverse this trend. Hopefully, an end to the footcandle syndrome will reveal the qualitative trade-off value and environmental enrichment potential inherent in sacrificing footcandles for the dynamics of coloured illumination. Its application to affect perceptual, emotional, and psychic responses to spaces designed for activities in which high degrees of visual acuity are neither necessary, desirable, nor appropriate, promises to be a major dividend from this alternative to prevailing illumination engineering practice (see figs. 81–3).

The Significance of Light and Colour in the Urban Environment

Faber Birren

The lighting industry today is seriously devoted to the development of sources that will duplicate light as encountered in average temperature zones and during most of the day. This light is generally judged as appearing neutral white or bluish, but the pink and orange light of dawn and dusk together with the yellow light of the sun are also constituents of natural light. In arctic regions, months will pass during which daylight remains constantly pink or orange and never white.

In nature, dim light such as we see at sunrise and sunset is usually warm and golden in hue as is firelight or candlelight. As daylight increases in intensity, it shifts from tints of pink to orange, to yellow and finally into white or even blue. Throughout these daylight colour-shifts the colours of objects will continue to be perceived as normal, i.e. no observer will find the changing scene to be unnatural. In effect, however, white or daylight illumination at low levels will cast an eerie pallor over the world, whereas warm light at the same levels will seem wholly proper. Thus for the sake of good appearances, warm illumination at low levels and cooler light at bright levels should be the aim; this follows nature's own example.

Rhythms of light and dark are entirely natural to man's experience. Lightness and darkness cause different physiological reactions in the body such as changes in body temperature. The action of light may also induce the secretion of hormones into the blood stream. With animals, including man, it is apparent that light and life are synonymous. Studies have indicated that radiant energy can actually penetrate into the mammalian brain. The researcher, E. D. Brunt, caused light to penetrate the skulls of sheep, dogs and rabbits. He demonstrated that, in a variety of mammalian species, light reaches the hypothalmus at the base of the brain — that part of the brain which is said to control vital autonomic nerve centres and fibres which, in turn, control such functions as respiration, heart action, digestion, etc.

A leading lighting engineer, H. L. Logan, has studied the effect of light on human beings. He points out that light dilates the blood vessels and increases circulation. Haemoglobin in the blood will be increased by light and decreased by darkness. Logan writes, 'We are natural creatures originating in the subtropics, attuned to high levels of natural illumination. We can operate for less, for a penalty — poorer health, shorter life expectancy.' It has been shown that sudden exposure to bright light stimulates the adrenal gland. There is, indeed, a time clock within all men that is regulated by day-night rhythms. R. J. Wurtman of M.I.T. states, 'These cycles synchronize a large number of biological rhythms.' The stimulation of light may come through the eyes but it may also trigger effects through the skin and subcutaneous tissues.

Most artificial environments today expose man to unbalanced light sources. Incandescent light is almost completely lacking in ultra-violet wavelengths. The glass tubes of most fluorescent lighting fixtures absorb and screen out ultra-violet. Some mercury sources, rich in ultra-violet, lack red and infra-red frequencies. Clear mercury lighting, however, is objectionable because of the environmental colour distortion and the ugly appearance of the human complexion.

The current need in artificial light perhaps comes down to ultra-violet and how much of it should be given to man for a beneficial result. Too much of it may result in a vitamin D deficiency. However, a measure of ultra-violet light is undoubtedly needed in artificial environments and sources emitting it are now being made. The Russians have been using ultra-violet radiation for years, in order to supplement conventional fluorescent lights in schools, hospitals and offices. In schools, learning ability is improved and catarrhal infections are fewer.

90

According to a report of the International Commission for Illumination, 'the action of ultra-violet radiation intensifies enzymatic processes of metabolism, increases the activity of the endocrine system, promotes the immunobiological responsiveness of the body and improves the tone of the central nerve and muscular system.' Parenthetically, it may be noted that while favourable to living things, ultra-violet can damage works of art, pigments, dyestuffs and textiles. It thus may be good for schools but not for museums and art galleries.

The artificial environment can be properly illuminated to help man's physical well-being but it is more than light alone that he needs. What about colour? There is a man of moods, feelings, emotions and he is not just someone who stands there and lets light penetrate his eyes, tissue and skull. It seems apparent from the many behavioural studies that all living things have a radiation sense. What is significant is that such sense may be independent of conscious vision itself. Awareness of the existence of light is noted in completely blind animals, even where heat and ultra-violet energy are excluded.

Reactions to colour through the eye itself are many, varied and intriguing. Generally, colour effects tend to be in two directions—towards red and towards blue—with the yellow and yellow-green regions of the spectrum more or less neutral. Further, these two major colours induce different levels of activation both in the autonomic nervous system and in the brain. Red seems to excite. Kurt Goldstein wrote, 'It is probably not a false statement if we say that a specific colour stimulation is accompanied by a specific response pattern in the entire organism.' Referring to red, he mentions the case of a woman with a cerebellar disease who had a tendency to fall unexpectedly. When she wore a red dress, such symptoms were more pronounced. Goldstein points out that such symptoms 'can be diminished if the individuals are protected against red or yellow, if they wear, for instance, spectacles with green lenses'.

There is a general light tonus in the muscular reactions of the human body; conditions of muscular tension and relaxation are noticeable and measurable. Outstretched arms tend to move towards red and away from green and blue. Goldstein concludes, 'The stronger deviation of the arms in red stimulation corresponds to the experience of being disrupted, thrown out, abnormally attracted to the outer world. It is only another expression of the patient's feelings of obtrusion, aggression, excitation, by red. The diminution of the deviation to green illumination corresponds to the withdrawal from the outer world and retreat into his own quietness, his centre. The inner experiences represent the psychological aspect of the reactions to the organism. We are faced in the observable phenomena with the physical aspect.'

It thus may be generalized that colour affects muscular tension, cortical activation (brain waves), heart rate, respiration and other functions of the autonomic nervous system, and certainly it arouses definite emotional and aesthetic associations.

An aesthetic approach has dominated the use of colour by architects and interior designers more or less since the beginning of time. Any judgements of colour on an artistic basis must be purely personal and arbitrary. Perhaps some people have a better sense of colour than others, but who is to know? It really doesn't make much difference what colours are used and how much originality and creative talent are shown if the particular space or environment is one in which the emotional factors of beauty can be allowed to prevail, as in a home, hotel, theatre or shop. But to let individual notions of beauty serve as criteria in other facilities, such as offices, schools or hospitals, where people are supposed to busy themselves at useful tasks or have their welfare regarded, is to take a supercilious attitude towards humanity.

One example of such indifference is found in the specification of white walls in offices. At high levels of illumination and with white walls all too often further washed with light, irreparable damage is being done to countless eyes. Perhaps white walls are attractive on casual inspection and allow for the dramatic use of accents on equipment and furnishings, but at what sacrifice? A few decades ago, two authorities on vision, C. E. Ferree and Gertrude Rand, wrote: 'The presence of high brilliances in the field of view produces a strong incentive for the eyes to fixate and accommodate for them, which incentive must be controlled by voluntary effort. The result of this opposition of voluntary control against strong reflex incentive is to tire the eye quickly and to make it lose the power to sustain the precision of adjustment needed for clear seeing of the work.' Ophthalmologists are in agreement. White glare, as a form of artificial snow blindness, can cause congestions in the eye, inflammation and scotoma. It can aggravate muscular imbalance, refractive difficulties, near-sightedness and astigmatism—perhaps not in a day or a week but over a prolonged period. It is doubtful if many architects or interior designers know of this fact.

With the advent of psychic lighting a good part of man's environment may well be due for a revolutionary change. When change comes, light and colour will be a vital part of it. What is significant here is that a 'simulation' of mind-expanding states can be induced; one does not have to take halucinogens. Turn up the lights, the colours and the sounds, and people can be emotionally transported. Barriers are broken down, and somehow people have less shyness and timidity. There is a good chance that psychic lighting may become one of the important, functional and rewarding contributions of the future artificial environment. The day is coming fast when even the most conservative and austere environment will be given more life and vitality through the introduction of psychic lighting in some form or another. In an office, factory or school, daylight sources plus some ultra-violet may be utilized for a good part of the day. Light and colour affects and perhaps even the projection of patterns and scenes will be monitored electronically for morning, noon, evening and night, just as in nature. Some of the light will be programmed for physiological well-being, some for emotional stability. Natural day and night cycles and rhythms will keep man attuned to harmonies with nature which have guided and controlled man's existence over aeons of time.

(2) Colour Preferences

In 1941 Hans Eysenck carried out an investigation into colour preference and, based on the results of his study, suggested the following order of general preference: (1) blue, (2) red, (3) green, (4) violet, (5) orange, (6) yellow. He then combined his findings with those of a larger number of previous international studies involving a total of 21,060 subjects of different race, age and cultural background and found the same result. This order, he suggested, was the 'universal scale' of colour preference. Eysenck also suggested that there was some strong biological basis for colour preference in that short wavelengths are generally preferred to long-wavelength colours. His suggestion concurs with that of J. P. Guilford who, in 1933, said 'There remains sufficient agreement upon colour preferences to indicate a basic biological cause of likes and dislikes for colour.'

Other findings show that there is some evidence that, in their first year, babies are fascinated by bright, long-wavelength colours while muted or short-wavelength colours hold little interest. Agreement also exists in research findings which suggest that up till the age of six the reds, oranges and yellows are preferred to the cool colours. It is also claimed that as children grow older, the preference for red changes until this is a positive liking for blue. If this is so, the transitional period coincides with the first psycho-physiological change in a child's life at seven (the period of change in the teeth).

Tom Porter carried out a series of tests with young children between the ages of five and nine using six coloured stimuli — red, orange, yellow, green, blue and violet — each colour-controlled along the dimensions of saturation and brightness. The results, although not statistically significant, did show an overwhelming liking for red up to the age of seven, the eight- and nine-year-olds indicating a preference for blue. Using Piaget's theory of the chronological stages of development, the change from long- to short-wavelength colour preference seems to occur after the 'egocentric stage' (between two and five years) and possibly coincides with his third developmental stage of 'incipient co-operation' between the ages of seven and eight.

Porter also tested in the eighteen to twenty-five age-range but a statistical analysis of the results showed little of significance. However, observations made of the use of six identical reading rooms painted in the six colours did indicate a liking for the violet space which coincided with a fashion for purple at that time (1973). On the assumption that African students in the same age group might be less exposed to fashionable colour trends, and in an attempt to ascertain the extent to which cultural background might influence colour preferences, two tests were conducted in Botswana and Kenya. The combined results from forty subjects were statistically significant: (1) blue and green, (3) violet, (4) orange, (5) red, (6) yellow.

Allowing for the importance of exposure to fashions in colour, the universal order is backed by a close relation between the African ranking and the results of an experiment with sixty- to ninety-year-old subjects by Porter in Oxford. The findings from this age-group may point to a seemingly established order of preference at a high level of agreement, the descending order of preference of forty subjects was: green, blue, violet, red, yellow and orange.

An interesting and, perhaps, contributory point about colour vision in the old is the fact that there is a process of deterioration of the eye with age. This occurs in the form of a 'skin' which produces a greying effect on the perception of colour and makes for difficulty in discrimination between green and blue. The test, however, showed these two hues as the most preferred colours and one might assume that they indicate agreement of an established liking for short wavelengths or that the ageing eye is seeking 'peace' in the passive colours — the blue and green hues possibly being perceived as neutrals. A question is raised when one begins to consider the application of such findings. Can we assume that preferred colours are necessarily the same colours that subjects would choose for their own living spaces? If this were the case, then a second question is raised. If preferred colours were applied to the interior of, say, an old people's home in the form of harmonizing combinations of blue and green, we might discover that failure to discriminate between these hues could lead to accidents. It seems paradoxical to find that the colours which are most likely to be confused by the aged were those which our test found to be most popular.

In summary, Porter tentatively suggests that an order of preference, if universal, might be even more closely related to the spectral arrangement of colour and that it might, in some age-groups or societies, be altered temporarily by the effect of external influences.

However, the fact that colours are not normally restricted to small, well-defined areas or perceived in isolation (as presented in most experiments) has led to some investigations into the more difficult area of contextual situations and colour combinations. Testing colours in real contexts is complicated and responses can relate partly to the qualities of individual colours and partly to the relationships between colours. Martin Lindauer, of the State University of New York, applied some findings produced by James Hogg (University of Manchester) on basic attitudes to colours in national flags. He found that the favourite colours were red, then blue followed by green and yellow. He concluded that the ideal flag, representing a composite picture of present findings, would be red and blue.

There appear to have been two kinds of investigations into colour preference. The original studies which postulate a biological order of preference related to wavelength were concerned more with hue than with saturation and brightness. The more recent work conducted by Carl-Axel Acking, Rikard Küller and Lars Sivik in Sweden investigated the dimensions of saturation and brightness using semantic differential techniques. They find no significant order of preference but claim that any liking was not based on a response to hue but to the brightness and saturation dimensions. Küller has stated that 'although some people believe the opposite, there is no direct correspondence between the colour experience and wavelength.' However, in the centre of this controversy some interest is revived in the biological order of preference suggested by Guilford and Eysenck in the light of some experiments with rhesus monkeys conducted by Dr N. K. Humphrey at the Universities of Oxford (1970) and Cambridge (1973).

The Colour Currency of Nature

Dr Nicholas Humphrey

Man as a species has little reason to boast about his sensory capacities. A dog's sense of smell, a bat's hearing, a hawk's visual acuity are all superior to man's own. But in one respect he may justifiably be vain: his ability to see colours is a match for any other animal. In this respect he has in fact surprisingly few rivals. Among mammals only his nearest relatives, the monkeys and apes, share his ability—all others are nearly or completely colour-blind. In the animal kingdom as a whole colour vision occurs only in some fishes, reptiles, insects and birds.

No one reading this book can doubt man's good fortune. The world seen in monochrome would be altogether a drearier, less attractive place to live in. But nature did not grant colour vision to man and other animals simply to indulge their aesthetic sensibilities. The ability to see colour can only have evolved because it contributes to biological survival.

The question of how colour vision has evolved is—or should be—an important issue for psychologists (and for designers). If we were to understand how the seeing of natural colour has in the distant past contributed to man's life we might be better placed to appreciate what colour in 'artificial' situations means to him. Yet it is not in fact an issue which has been much explored. Indeed, few psychologists, for all their obsession with the physiological mechanism of colour vision, have asked what to an evolutionary biologist must seem the obvious question: where — and *why* — does colour occur in nature?

It may seem odd to tack 'why' on to the question 'where?' But the question *why* is crucial, for the evolution of colour vision is intimately linked to the evolution of colour on the surface of the Earth. It may go without saying that in a world without colour animals would have no use for colour vision; but it does need saying that in a world without animals possessing colour vision there would in fact be very little colour. The variegated colours which characterize the Earth's surface (and make the Earth perhaps the most colourful planet of the universe) are in the main *organic* colours, carried by the tissues of plants and animals—and most of these life-born colours have been designed in the course of evolution to be *seen*.

There are of course exceptions. Before life evolved the drab landscape of the Earth may have been relieved occasionally by, say, a volcanic fire, a rainbow, a sunset, perhaps some tinted crystals on the ground. And before colour vision evolved some living tissues were already 'fortuitously' coloured—blood was red, foliage green, although the redness of haemoglobin and the greenness of chlorophyll are wholly incidental to their biochemical roles. But the most striking colours of nature, those of flowers and fruits, the plumage of birds, the gaudy fishes of a coral reef, are all 'deliberate' evolutionary creations which have been selected to act as visual *signals* carrying messages to those who have the eyes to see them. The pigments which impart visible colour to the petals of a dandelion or a robin's breast are there for no other purpose.

We may presume that colour vision has not evolved to see the rare colours of inorganic nature, since rainbows and sunsets have no importance to survival. Nor is it likely to have evolved to see simply the greenness of grass or the redness of raw flesh, since those animals which feed chiefly on grass or on flesh are colour-blind. It can and almost surely has evolved alongside signal coloration to enable animals to detect and interpret nature's colour-coded messages.

The messages conveyed by signal coloration are of many kinds. Sometimes the message is simple: 'come here' addressed to an ally (the colour of a flower serving to attract a pollinating insect, the colour of a fruit to attract a seed-dispersing bird), or 'keep away' addressed to an enemy (the colour of a stinging insect or a poisonous toadstool serving to deter a potential predator). Sometimes the message is more complex, as when colour is used for communication in a social context in courtship or aggressive encounters (a peacock displaying his fan, a monkey flashing his coloured genitalia). Whatever the level of the message, signal colours commonly have three functions: they catch attention, they transmit information, and they directly affect the emotions of the viewer—an orange arouses appetite in a monkey, a yellow wasp fear in a fly-catcher, the red lips of a young woman passion in a man.

Primates come on the scene relatively late in evolutionary history, and the surface of the Earth must already have been given much of its colour through the interaction of plants, insects, reptiles and birds. The early tree-dwelling primates moved in on an ecological niche previously occupied by birds: they picked the same fruits, caught the same insects, and they were in danger of being harmed by the same stings and the same poisons. To compete effectively with birds, primates needed to evolve colour vision of the same order. It is for that reason, I suspect, that the trichromatic colour vision of most primates (including man) is in fact so similar to that, say, of a pigeon (although, as it happens, the selectivity of the three types of colour receptor is achieved by quite different physiological mechanisms in primates and birds). Once primates had joined the colour vision club, however, they too must have played their part in the progressive evolution of natural colour, influencing through selection the colours both of themselves and of other plants and animals.

Then, not far back in history, the emergence of man marked a turning point in the use of colour. For men hit on a new and unique skill—the ability to *apply* colour in places where it did not *grow*. Most probably they first used artificial colour to adorn their own bodies, painting their skins, investing themselves with jewels and feathers, dressing in coloured clothes. But in time they went further and began to apply colour to objects around them, especially to things which they themselves had made . . . until the use of colour became eventually almost a trademark of the human species.

In the early stages men probably continued the natural tradition of using colour primarily for its signal function, to indicate maybe status or value. And to some extent this tradition has continued to the present day, as testified for instance, in the use we make of colour in ceremonial dress, traffic signals, political emblems, or the rosettes awarded to horses at a show. But at the same time the advent of modern technology has brought with it a debasement of the colour currency. Today almost every object that rolls off the factory production line, from motor cars to pencils, is given a distinctive colour—and for the most part these colours are *meaningless*. As I look around the room I'm working in, man-made colour shouts back at me from every surface: books, cushions, a rug on the floor, a coffee cup, a box of staples—bright blues, reds, yellows, greens. There is as much colour here as in any tropical forest. Yet whilst almost every colour in the forest would be meaningful, here in my study almost nothing is. Colour anarchy has taken over.

The indiscriminate use of colour has no doubt dulled man's biological response to it. From the first moment that a baby is given a string of multi-coloured—but otherwise identical—beads to play with he is unwittingly being taught to *ignore* colour as a signal. Yet I do not believe that our long involvement with colour as a signal in the course of evolution can be quite forgotten. Though modern man's use of colour may frequently be arbitrary, his response to it continues to show traces of his evolutionary heritage. So men persist in seeking meaning from colour even where no meaning is intended: they find colour attention-catching, they expect colour to carry information and to some extent at least they tend to be emotionally aroused.

The most striking illustration of man's biological inheritance is the significance which is attached to the colour *red*. I was first alerted to the peculiar psychological importance of red by some experiments not on men but on rhesus monkeys. For some years I have been studying the visual preferences of monkeys, using the apparatus shown in the illustration (fig. 100). The monkey sits in a dark testing chamber with a screen at one end on to which one of two alternative slides can be projected. The monkey controls the presentation of the slides by pressing a button, each press producing one or the other slide in strict alternation: thus when he likes what he sees he must hold the button down, when he wants a change he must release and press again. I examined 'colour preference' in this situation by letting the monkeys choose between two plain fields of coloured light. All the monkeys which were tested showed strong and consistent preferences. When given a choice between, for instance, red and blue, they tended to spend three or four times as long with the blue as the red. Overall, the rank order of colours in order of preference was blue, green, yellow, orange, red. When each of the colours was separately paired with a 'neutral' white field, red and orange stood out as strongly aversive, blue and green as mildly attractive. Direct observation of the monkeys in the testing situation indicated that they were considerably upset by the red light. When I deliberately added to their stress by playing loud and unpleasant background noise throughout the test, the aversion to red light became even more extreme. Further experiments showed that they were reacting to the red light exactly as if it was inducing fear.

This aversion to red light is not unique to rhesus monkeys. The same thing has been found with baboons and also, more surprisingly, with pigeons. But what about men? Experiments on colour preference in men have given results which appear at first sight to be at odds with those in other primates. When men are asked to rank colours according to how much they 'like' them red often comes high if not top of the list, although there is a wide variation between individuals depending among other things on personality, age, sex and culture. I am inclined to give little weight to such findings for two reasons. First, as Tom Porter has emphasized, the choice of a 'favourite' colour may be heavily biased by changes in fashion; indeed, when Porter tested people from social backgrounds where fashion probably has relatively little influence — African children on the one hand, the residents of an Oxford Old People's Home on the other—he found that both groups ranked colours in much the same way as did my monkeys, consistently preferring the blue end of the spectrum to the red (Porter 1973). Second, and more important, there is a methodological problem with most of the preference experiments, for the question 'which do you *like* best?' is really much too simple a question to ask of a man; men may say they 'like' a colour for a host of different reasons depending both on the context in which they imagine the colour occurring and on how they construe the term 'like'. It would be manifestly silly to ask people the abstract question 'do you like better to be excited or to be soothed?' and it may perhaps be equally silly to ask 'do you like red more than blue?' To discover the significance of colours to man we must look to rather more specific studies.

I shall list briefly some of the particular evidence which demonstrates how, in a variety of contexts, red seems to have a very special significance for man. (1) Large fields of red light induce physiological symptoms of emotional arousal—changes in heart rate, skin resistance and the electrical activity of the brain. (2) In patients suffering from certain pathological disorders, for instance cerebellar palsy, these physiological effects become exaggerated—in cerebellar patients red light may cause intolerable distress, exacerbating the disorders of posture and movement, lowering pain thresholds and causing a general disruption of thought and skilled behaviour. (3) When the affective value of colours is measured by a technique, the 'semantic differential', which is far subtler than a simple preference test, men rate red as a 'heavy', 'powerful', 'active', 'hot' colour. (4) When the 'apparent weight' of colours is measured directly by asking men to find the balance point between two discs of colour, red is consistently judged to be the heaviest. (5) In the evolution of languages, red is without exception the first colour word to enter the vocabulary—in a study of ninety-six languages Berlin and Kay (1969) found thirty in which the only colour word (apart from black and white) was red. (6) In the development of a child's language red again usually comes first, and when adults are asked simply to reel off colour words as fast as they can they show a very strong tendency to start with red. (7) When colour vision is impaired by central brain lesions, red vision is most resistant to loss and quickest to recover.

These disparate facts all point the same way, to the conclusion that man as a species finds red both a uniquely impressive colour and at times a uniquely disturbing one. Why should it be so? What special place does the colour red have in nature's scheme of colour signals?

The explanation of red's psychological impact must surely be that red is by far the most common colour signal in nature. There are two good reasons why red should be chosen to send signals. First, by virtue of the contrast it provides, red stands out peculiarly well against a background of green foliage or blue sky. Second, red happens to be the colour most readily available to animals for colouring their bodies because, by pure chance, it is the colour of blood. So an animal can create an effective signal simply by bringing to the surface of its body the pigment already flowing through its arteries: witness the cock's comb, the red bottom of a monkey in heat, the blush of a woman's cheek.

The reason why red should be in certain situations so disturbing is more obscure. If red was always used as a warning signal there would be no problem. But it is not, it is used as often to attract as to repel. My guess is that its potential to disturb lies in this very *ambiguity* as a signal colour. Red toadstools, red ladybirds, red poppies are dangerous to eat, but red tomatoes, red strawberries, red apples are good. The open red mouth of an aggressive monkey is threatening, but the red bottom of a sexually receptive female is appealing. The flushed cheeks of a man or woman may indicate anger, but they may equally indicate pleasure. Thus the colour red, of itself, can do no more than alert the viewer, preparing him to receive a potentially important message; the content of the message can be interpreted only when the *context* of the redness is defined. When red occurs in an unfamiliar context it becomes therefore a highly risky colour. The viewer is thrown into conflict as to what to do. All his instincts tell him to do *something,* but he has no means of knowing what that something ought to be. No wonder that my monkeys, confronted by a bright red screen, became tense and panicky: the screen shouts at them 'this is important', but without a framework for interpretation they are unable to assess what the import is. And no wonder that human subjects in the artificial, contextless situation of a psychological laboratory may react in a similar way. A West African tribe, the Ndembu, state the dilemma explicitly, 'red acts both for good and evil' . . . it all depends.

I have tried to show how an evolutionary approach can help throw light on man's response to colour. Whether this approach can be helpful to the practice of design remains an open question. In many areas of our lives we already overrule and nullify man's natural tendencies. But I believe we should try to be 'conservationists' as much on behalf of ourselves as we are learning to be on behalf of other species, and that we should try where possible to make our style of life conform to the style to which man is biologically adapted. Designers, who are now more than anyone responsible for colouring our world, have a choice before them. They can continue to devalue colour by using it in an arbitrary, non-natural way, or they can recognize and build on man's biological predisposition to treat colour as a signal. If they choose the latter, bolder course they might do well to study how colour is used in nature. Nature has, after all, been in the business of design for over a hundred million years.

(3) The Effect of Colour on our Perception of Space

'The exterior volume of an architecture, its sensitive weight, its distance, can be reduced or increased as a result of the colours adopted.' Fernand Léger

A large number of studies have been conducted during this century which have attempted to determine the effect of colour on our perception of space and time. In these experiments, colour has been investigated as an independent factor and measured in terms of observer's judgements of weight, temperature, depth and size. Included in Leonardo da Vinci's manuscripts are many references to the behaviour of colour in space, and on changes in apparent size of colours he wrote: 'A dark object seen against a light background will seem smaller than it is. A light object will appear greater in size when it is seen against a background that is darker in colour.' In reference to apparent depth in the figure-ground context he commented, 'Of colours of equal whiteness that will seem most dazzling which is on the darkest background, and black will seem most intense when it is against a background of greater whiteness. Red also will seem most vivid when against a yellow background, and so in like manner with all the colours when set against those which present the sharpest contrast.'

Painters consciously manipulate the apparent weight of colours, and their paintings are often said to have a centre of gravity which is possibly determined by colour juxtaposition. Edward Bullough, in 1907, first experimented with this particular aspect of colour perception by asking his subjects to judge, or balance, small coloured paper circles located at either end of a simulated balance arm with an adjustable fulcrum. His subjects generally agreed that red and blue were the heaviest colours and that yellow appeared to be the lightest. In 1925 Marion Monroe conducted a similar test and her findings, together with those of several other investigators, reported that the apparent heaviness of colour varied with the brightness level of the coloured stimuli rather than hue — in other words, the brighter the colour the lighter it was perceived.

However, no statistical evaluation was employed in the early studies and as their coloured stimuli were surface illuminated, the effect of colour was probably confused with its brightness.

A recent study by Dr. N. Humphrey and Elizabeth Pinkerton (1974) adapted the balance arm-adjustable fulcrum test procedure and investigated the effect of colour and brightness separately, using larger, transilluminated stimuli, with brightness carefully controlled. Their findings indicate that the apparent heaviness of colour is independent of brightness. Colour circles, equal in subjective brightness, differ considerably in apparent weight, while achromatic stimuli which vary in brightness are not consistently different in weight. In the test, yellow was judged as appearing significantly lighter than all the other colours presented, and red was seen as significantly heavier than blue, green and orange — in that order. The results for brightness showed no significant effect of any kind.

Through a collation of all the previous study findings in the literature the authors have found a statistically significant order of apparent weight which, reading from heavy to light, is as follows: red, blue, purple, orange, green, yellow. However, the influence of colour on heaviness as judged by actual lifting seems slight, if at all significant.

Many of the early studies into the effects of apparent colour temperature agree that as hue moves from red to blue, apparent temperature moves from warm to cool. However, in 1960 P. C. Berry conducted an experiment in which subjects in a car simulator were led to believe that effects of coloured illumination on driving performance was being studied when the real test was on the effects of colour in apparent temperature. The subjects were instructed to push a button when the temperature of the space rose to a point at which they felt uncomfortably warm. The temperature of the simulator was gradually changed, but the changes were the same for each of the five colours of diffuse illumination: green, blue, yellow, amber and white. The brightness of each illuminant was the same. This experiment found that there was no significant difference between apparent levels of discomfort between the colours of illumination. However, when the subjects were later asked to order the five colours according to the amount of heat they transmitted, the result was significant. Green and blue were ranked almost identically as the coolest; white was placed at an intermediate position, and yellow and amber were ranked almost identically as warmer. Thus subjects persisted in the conventional belief that green and blue are cool hues, although in the simulator they did not experience them any differently from other colours in the levels of heat the subjects would tolerate.

In 1962 Benjamin Wright, using the semantic differential scale, found support for the conventional concept of colour temperature. His report suggested that effects of brightness and saturation were less definitive than those for hue, but increasing warmth ratings did, to an extent, correspond with increasing saturation. This is generally confirmed by other experimental studies (S. C. Newhall, 1941; T. Kimura, 1950, etc.) which regularly show various reds and yellows to provide the warmest impressions and blues and greens the coolest.

Two explanations have been offered for the illusion of depth generated by certain colours: the first suggests that apparent depth is caused by chromatic aberration (S. H. Bartley, 1958). This aberration, in the refractive media of the eye radiation of short wavelengths, causes images to be focused within the eye closer to the lens than the radiation of long wavelengths. Bartley suggests a similar kind of effect appears for distance, as distant objects project images closer to the lens than near-by objects. Thus, a red object would appear to be closer than an identical blue object perceived at the same distance. The second explanation is related to Leonardo da Vinci's observations of the figure-ground interaction. In his paper 'Visual Space Perception' (1960), W. H. Ittleson refers to the work of W. M. Smith: the more a colour approximates its background, the more it appears to recede towards the background and, conversely, the more a colour differs from its background the nearer it seems.

A paper entitled 'The Long and Short of Colour Distance', and presented in 1960 by Randall M. Hanes, contradicts the popular 'rule of thumb' application of advancing warm colours and receding cool colours to architectural settings. He compared judgements gained from subjects located in an experimental room with an adjustable end wall, against results from a post-test questionnaire which asked the same subjects to order eight colours from most to least advancing. In the adjustable room, yellow and green were judged as the most advancing with black seen as the least advancing; white occupied fourth position. The questionnaire produced the more conventional order: red and black were rated as being the most advancing, and white the least. The fact that his experiment was conducted in a real space, and that a white wall was perceived as nearer than a black wall, although both were located at the same actual distance from the observer, prompted him to question the generally held belief that a white room would appear as 'larger' than a black one.

However, almost all the evidence from studies in the field verify that the brightness dimension of colour appears to be the cue for its psychological alignment with our perception of depth.

The interaction between apparent depth and apparent size is well known. The fact that a lighter object appears to be nearer and larger than a darker object of the same size and perceived at the same physical distance is simply an example of this interaction. Studies by W. Bevan and W. F. Dukes (1953), R. Sato (1955), and J. C. Franklin (1956) found brightness to be significantly correlated with apparent size — brighter objects being overestimated.

100

In discussing the role of colour in our perception of space it is interesting to note the discrepancy between the data, particularly in relation to apparent temperature and apparent depth, from experiments conducted in real space and those conducted in the laboratory. In both the Berry and the Hanes study subjects made synaesthetic judgements in 'architectural' situations and their results contradicted both conventional concepts of spatial colour behaviour and laboratory findings at large. This, and the fact that our perception of colour-space has been described in terms of stimulus cues and treated as independent variables, points to the need for the interaction and the interdependence of these and other variables to be studied and explained in real environments. For this reason we present in the next chapter the colour experiments which have been validated in the architectural environment.

Meanwhile, the needs of spaceflight have demanded a design criterion for working and living situations in outer space. Advanced space research has established the need to combat problems arising from 'sensory deprivation' in extraterrestrial environments and proposals for the creation of warmth and well-being include the application of textures, patterns, light and colour which might induce associations with home and Earth. To this end, it is suggested that imitation rocks and plants together with simulated natural finishes (wood, stone, bricks, etc.) and murals could be introduced. Their colour proposals, based on data derived from man-machine environment studies and the work of Kurt Goldstein and Faber Birren, summarize the general findings from colour research at large in their proposed application to extraterrestrial interior design.

The Study and Application of Colour in Extraterrestrial Habitats

National Aeronautics and Space Administration, Johnson Spacecraft Centre, Houston, Texas

A short presentation of colour proposals for application to artificial and zero-gravity environments, based on the collective findings together with studies carried out in mock-ups and simulators, and prepared by the Habitability Technology Section at the Manned Spacecraft Centre.

Habitability has a long history of being the last considered, and the first to be compromised, in most of man's endeavours in man-machine environments. However, for a man to live and work in outer space for extended periods of time, greater emphasis is being placed on his comfort and the visual quality of his environment.

Beyond the Mercury, Gemini and Apollo missions, in which the astronaut primarily supplemented the capability of his spacecraft and where environmental features were minimal, the advent of longer duration voyages will require him to play a more complex role. The National Aeronautics and Space Administration have, therefore, investigated the quality of artificial habitats with considered seriousness. It has been established by them that the characteristics of an extraterrestrial environment, be it space vehicle or station, should gravitate toward or simulate the same basic format as our present-day terrestrial life style.

The investigation and use of colour in space system design is, therefore, seen as necessary in helping to provide visual stimulation, volume enhancement, and in creating moods in order to relieve the monotony of prolonged confinement. Colour was studied as an important architectural element in artificial and zero-gravity environments and in interaction with the factors of lighting, texture, design patterns and safety. Colour schemes are planned in relation to room volume and function, purpose of the mission and desired behavioural aspects.

The association of colours with definite mental conditions and moods is general. No absolute relationships have been established, and the subject is open to individual interpretation. However, research has shown that certain general reactions are common to most people and the following tables represent the broad picture of findings in relation to the psychological aspects of colours; they are used as basic guidelines for the interior design of extraterrestrial living and working spaces:

A study of the interrelationships of colour with odours and tastes suggest that pink, lavender, pale yellow and green hold pleasant associations with odours. The tints of coral, peach, soft yellow and light green and the richer colours of vermilion, flamingo, pumpkin and turquoise have pleasant associations with taste. The application of any of these colours in food preparation areas has been shown to facilitate appetite appeal.

An example of the problem of individual differences in habitability concerns the use of colour in living areas. Personal preference depends upon such factors as the individual's familiarity with certain colours and colour combinations and the emotional connotations, either conscious or subconscious, that they may have for him. It is generally assumed that emotionally responsive persons will react freely to colour, inhibited individuals will feel uneasy with an actively coloured environment, and restricted or detached types may be unaffected. Most good colour schemes, however, consist of no more than three hues and the use of warm or cool colours is determined by the function of the roomspace involved. Warm hues are associated with extraverted responses and feelings and they should be used in spaces where it would be beneficial to emphasize feelings of extraversion (e.g., an area in

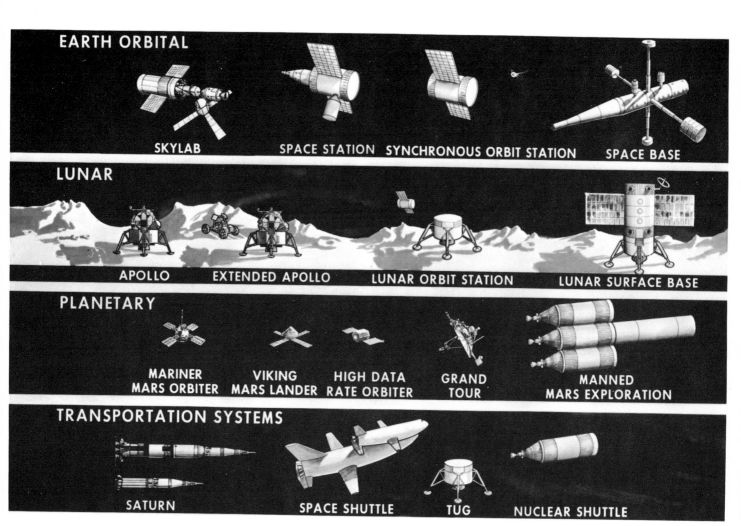

EARTH ORBITAL

SKYLAB   SPACE STATION   SYNCHRONOUS ORBIT STATION   SPACE BASE

LUNAR

APOLLO   EXTENDED APOLLO   LUNAR ORBIT STATION   LUNAR SURFACE BASE

PLANETARY

MARINER MARS ORBITER   VIKING MARS LANDER   HIGH DATA RATE ORBITER   GRAND TOUR   MANNED MARS EXPLORATION

TRANSPORTATION SYSTEMS

SATURN   SPACE SHUTTLE   TUG   NUCLEAR SHUTTLE

61
Systems for Space Exploration. (photo: copyright NASA)

1. Effects of Hue

EFFECT	HUE	CONTRAST
Exciting	Bright red Bright orange	High
Stimulating	Red Orange	Moderate
Cheering	Light orange Yellow Warm grey	Moderate
Neutralizing	Grey White/off-white	Low
Retiring	Cool grey Light green Light blue	Low
Relaxing	Blue Green	Low
Subduing	Purple	Moderate
Depressing	Black	Low

2. Brightness, Colour Saturation and Illumination Level Effects on the Perception of Volume

VOLUME (ROOMINESS)	BRIGHTNESS	COLOUR SATURATION	ILLUMINATION LEVEL
Enlarge	Areas will be enlarged by lightness and small patterns (use to alleviate feelings of oppression or 'closed-in').	Pale or desaturated colours 'recede'. In situations where equipment projects into a room and tends to make it appear smaller than it actually is, paint the projections the same colour as the ceiling or wall — a very light shade — to make them appear to recede into wall or ceiling.	High
Close-in	Areas will be closed-in by darkness and large patterns.	Dark or saturated hues 'protrude'.	Low

104

3. Colour Effects on Perception of Time, Size, Weight and Volume

COLOUR	PERCEPTION OF TIME	SIZE	WEIGHT	VOLUME
'Warm'	Time is over-estimated; use warm colours for areas where time in apparent 'slow motion' might be more pleasureable (eating, recreation).	Things seem longer and bigger.	Weights seem heavier.	Decreases apparent size of rooms.
'Cool'	Time is under-estimated; use cool colours for areas where routine or monotonous tasks are performed.	Things seem shorter and smaller.	Weights seem lighter. (Use on boxes & containers which must be carried about)	Increases apparent size of rooms.

4. Interrelationships in Living Areas

COLOUR	SOUND	TEMPERATURE	SUBJECTIVE IMPRESSION IN LIVING AREAS
'Warm'	Noise induces a hazier perception of warm colours. Brightness, loudness, stimulation of senses in general are associated with the most active effect of warm colours.	'Warmness' — use to soften up chilly or vaulty spaces	Centrifugal action — with high levels of illumination, warm and luminous colours, the person tends to direct attention outward. There is increased activation in general, alertness, outward orientation. Such an environment is conducive to muscular effort, action, and cheerfulness.
'Cool'	Noise increases sensitivity for cool colours. Dimness, quietness and sedation of the senses in general are associated with the most active effect of cool colours.	'Coolness' — use where working conditions expose person to warm temperatures.	Centripetal action — with softer surroundings, colour hues, and lower levels of illumination, there is less distraction and a person's ability to concentrate on difficult visual and mental tasks is enhanced. Good inward orientation is furthered.

61a
The use of colour in space system design is necessary in providing visual stimulation, volume enhancement, and in creating different moods to relieve the monotony of prolonged confinement. (photo: NASA)

106

which social contact is implicit to the function of the area — usage of warm hues will maximize these feelings; usage of cool colours will minimize them). Warm hues should generally be used if the temperature of the room is cool, the noise element is low, the room size is too large, texture is smooth, physical exertion is light, time exposure is short, a stimulating atmosphere is desired and the light sources are fluorescent (cool).

The introverted response is associated with cool hues and where a contemplative atmosphere is dictated by the function of the area, cool colours will add emphasis; warm hues will dilute this type of atmosphere. Cool hues should generally be applied when the temperature is warm, the noise element is high, room size is too small, texture is rough, physical exertion is heavy, time exposure is long, a restful atmosphere is desired and light sources are incandescent or fluorescent (warm).

Colour intensity induces two basic mental sets. A centrifugal mental set is one in which an individual's attention is directed outwards and high colour intensity and high levels of illumination as well as warm hues evoke this set to its highest degree. Conversely, the centripetal mental set directs an individual's attention inwards. Low colour intensity and low levels of lighting, as well as cool colours, maximize the centripetal mental set. As colour is greyed, the further it appears to be from the eye of the observer. Atmospheric perspective conditions the eye to perceive grey colours in this manner, and this natural phenomenon is retained by the observer in artificial environments; thus the control of brightness can be used to enlarge a space visually (see fig. 87).

The establishment of criteria in compiling architectural and environmental data was based on the consideration of the personnel first and the equipment second. A further important consideration is that designers should provide variety in the long-term spacecraft habitat by purposefully modifying colour with environmental features.

6 The Natural Colour System and its Application to Interior and Exterior Environments (the Swedish Studies)

An interest in colour and colour perception manifested itself several years ago in Sweden when Tryggve Johanssen introduced his version of Ewald Hering's theories (1878) concerning opponent colours and called it the Natural Colour System. Based on this work, Sven Hesselgren prepared a 'colour atlas' in the late forties which was published in 1952. 1964 saw the foundation of the Swedish Colour Centre which was established under the directorship of Anders Hård who, after a decade of dedicated work, has produced a new version of the Natural Colour System, the NCS, which is the experimental documentation of Hering's original theories and a practical tool for descriptive colour designations.

This research could have profound implications for designers in simplifying colour communication, specification and psychological findings. As an important means of developing future colour investigations the NCS can be used both in teaching and in environmental perception projects.

The studies of colour connotations included in this chapter are based on the theoretical standpoint of Charles Osgood's semantic differential approach (1957), which attempts to quantify the connotative meaning of concepts suiting such statistical methods as 'factor analysis'. This method has been employed extensively in architectural psychology research and, although it is not completely without criticism, even from its originator, several experimental projects have proved both interesting and rewarding.

As these experiments are amongst the first applications of the Natural Colour System the original dimension terms of the NCS are retained rather than the colour nomenclature used thus far in the book:

Hue is described in NCS terms as the degree of similarity of any colour to the four basic colour attributes: yellowness, redness, blueness and greenness. *Saturation* is described in terms of 'chromaticness' which means the degree of similarity to the most conceivable colour strength of a certain hue. *Brightness* has no directly comparable dimension in the Natural Colour System. The new version of the NCS describes each colour according to its visual similarity to whiteness and blackness. Black is signified by the letter s which represents the Swedish equivalent *Svart* (Swarthy).

108

The Natural Colour System and its Universal Application in the Study of Environmental Design

Anders Hård

When discussing colour as an environmental factor, it is essential to bear in mind that we are concerned with a two-stage procedure:
(1) The process in which human beings perceive colours and colour combinations.
(2) The effect of coloured pigments and materials on environmental perception.

A true knowledge of the interaction between colour perception and man is imperative if we are to formulate human requirements in environmental design. In its wider implications, this study is essential to the creators of our environment and to those industries which market coloured materials.

However, under the pressure of production, technology and physical science, colour has mainly been approached as a physical entity in spite of the fact that physics can only describe and specify spectral energy distribution with the help of measuring instruments, but does not measure what we *see*. Energy radiation is the stimulus correlated to colour perception but it is not the same as the colour experience.

In a very simple way this can be demonstrated in the following well-known experiment:

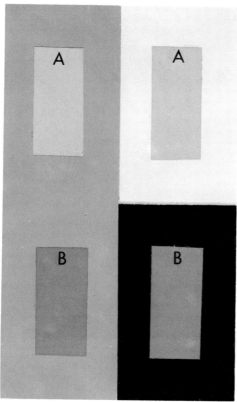

62
The difference between physical stimulus and perception. The light grey rectangle (A) against a white background appears the same as the darker grey (B) against a black background. We have, therefore, two different colour stimuli resulting in the same colour perception in different contexts.

Under technological influences, many so-called colour order systems have been developed as a means of measuring the colour stimulus and setting physical tolerances for the production of coloured materials. Both are essential in our technologically well-developed culture but they have little concern with our perception of environmental colour or reactions and behaviour in a coloured world.

It is not only the physicist who has contributed to the confusion between colour as perceived and colour stimuli as emitted (the same problem seems to exist when discussing light, sound, texture, etc.). Psychologists involved in psychophysical studies have also, very often, used physical approaches as the basis for perceptual investigations. Thus, the perceptual structure has been formed and biased by the physical 'truths' conceptually involved in their experiments. Among artists we also discover physically based theories of colour and colour combinations such as the aesthetic doctrine of the value of physically complementary colour stimuli.

In contrast to the classical, physically based studies, our phenomenological approach primarily begins with colours as *seen* and how they *appear* to be related to each other; only at a secondary stage does it attempt to specify the stimulus — the cause of the perception in one specific situation. This approach was devised by Ewald Hering who, in 1874, presented what he called the Natural Colour System. He named it thus, not because it was supposed to be the most natural method of arranging colour, but because he considered it conveyed a more precise explanation of human colour vision than the Young-Helmholtz Trichromatic theory.

From his phenomenological analysis, Hering postulated that we have six elementary colour experiences: white (w), black (s), yellow (y), red (r), blue (b) and green (g). All other colour perceptions are, characteristically, related to these elementary colours by various degrees of similarity to them. He also demonstrated that these relationships can be represented in a three-dimensional model — the colour solid. This can be represented by its two projections, the colour circle and the colour triangle.

At the Swedish Colour Centre Foundation we have worked since 1964 on a research and development project to experiment with Hering's theory and to quantify these similarities. After ten years of psychophysical research we are now capable of presenting a colour order and scaling system called the NCS. We have also developed a prototype colour atlas which, containing colour samples illustrating the NCS colour system, will meet the need for a vehicle for colour communication and as a tool for future colour research.

Apart from this application, Hering's phenomenological researches led to a physiological theory for colour vision known as the Opponent Theory. It is illustrated here using the Valraven-Vos model as an example.

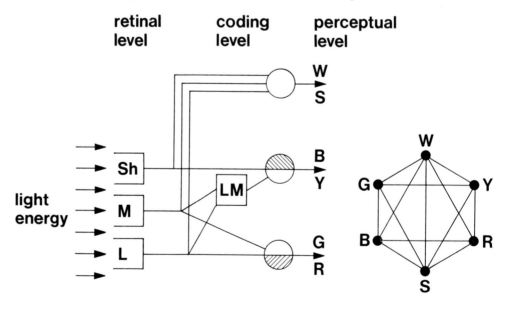

Learning the Natural Colour System

The NCS is a systematic method of describing the relationship between colours, purely from their perceptual qualities, which are the only properties that can be seen and evaluated with the help of the natural colour sense. It does not, and should not, use any knowledge concerning the attributes of materials (paint, dyes, inks, etc.) nor with physical radiation resulting from, say, colour 'mixing' such as Maxwell's discs.

The relationship between these six elementary colour perceptions can be described in a simple model:

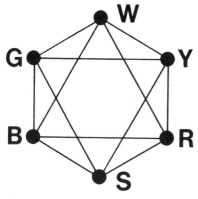
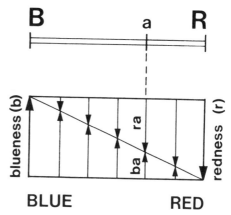

64

In this model, a line that connects two elementary colours, i.e., B – R describes a series of colours which continually vary from blue to red. From a pure blue, the colours become more and more reddish and end up in the pure red which contains no blue characteristic. This simultaneously increasing similarity with red (redness) and decreasing similarity with blue (blueness) was exemplified by Hering in a bi-polar diagram. In this, a specific proportion of blueness (ba) and redness (ra) is represented by a point (a) on the line from blue to red.

This method is the simplest way of showing how to quantify the similarity between two elementary colours. As we have six elementary colours, we have also to account for six similarities or attributes. The elementary colour attributes are called: whiteness (w), blackness (s), yellowness (y), redness (r), blueness (b), greenness (g). Thus, the single lines in the simplified model illustrate colours varying only in two attributes related to the elementary colours which form the end points of the scales. Now, one may ask, why is there no line linking green (G) and red (R) or yellow (Y) and blue (B). The answer is, of course, that as long as the model shows perceptual relationships between the elementary colours and, as long as one *cannot perceive* a greenish red or a bluish yellow, such a line would be incorrect.

This should not be confused with the knowledge that one can mix yellow pigment with blue pigment (subtractive mixture). Perceptually, this results in the yellow becoming more greenish and, not until the mix has reached the green, would one perceive some blueness in the green. Nor should the perceptual phenomenon be confused with what happens when one mixes the red and green signal in a colour television (additive mixture), which results in yellow.

For an arbitrary colour perception, the perceptual similarities to the elementary colours can be expressed in a very simple equation. The total similarity to an elementary colour is given the figure 100 — representing the degree of similarity to their elementary colour imagination:

(1) $s+w+y+r+b+g=100$

63 *(Opposite)*
Example of opponent theory colour vision. The varying wavelengths of electromagnetic radiation stimulates the retinal cones which are sensitive to short (sh), medium (M), and long (L) wavelength radiation. Next, at the coding level in the visual system, the radiations are recoded into signals resulting in blue or yellow; green or red; and black and white perception as seen in the right side of the diagram.

The sum of the chromatic attributes is called 'chromaticness' (c), and a colour where c=100 is called a maximal (chromatic) colour=c (all chromatic elementary colours and intermediaries with no traces of whiteness or blackness are maximal colours):

(2) y+r+b+g=c

From what has been said, it is also clear that no colour perception can simultaneously contain either yellowness and blueness or redness and greenness. From this very fact, these relationships (1) can be graphically illustrated in a three-dimensional colour solid and its two projections, the Colour Triangle and the Colour Circle (figs. 65–7).

In this way we have arrived at a logical colour notation with figures representing the three NCS parameters: s, c, ø.

Blackness	(s) = degree of similarity to black.
'Chromaticness'	(c) = degree of similarity to the maximal colour of a specific hue.
Hue	(ø) = relationship in two chromatic elementary attributes.

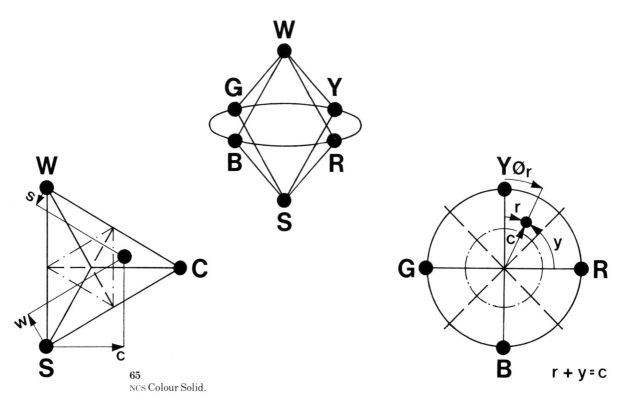

65
NCS Colour Solid.

66
NCS Colour Triangle
s + w + c = 100 (or) s + c = 100 − w.

67
NCS Colour Circle

$$ør=\frac{r}{y+r}.100=\frac{r}{c}.100 \qquad øb=\frac{b}{r+b}.100=\frac{b}{c}.100 \qquad øg=\frac{g}{b+g}.100=\frac{g}{c}.100 \qquad øy=\frac{y}{g+y}.100=\frac{y}{c}.100$$

thus ø represents a proportional specification of equalness to two chromatic elementary colours. (For actual colour see fig. 92.)

For the colour marked in the model (figs. 66, 67) we can identify:

(1) The similarity to black = blackness $s = 10$

(2) The similarity to white = whiteness $w = 30$

(3) The similarity to yellow = yellowness $y = 45$

(4) The similarity to red = redness $r = 15$ } $= c = 60$
$\overline{}$
100

(5) Hue ø r = $\dfrac{15}{45+15}$ .100 = 25

y+r perceived as the chromatic component ('chromaticness') i.e., similarity to maximum c which is 100. In our example c = 45 + 15 = 60, which means that the yellowness represents 75 per cent and redness 25 per cent of the 'chromaticness'. The NCS notation for this colour is: *1060 Y25R* in which —
10 represents 's'.
60 represents 'c'.
Y-R represents the yellow-red quadrant.
25 represents the proportion of 'r' in 'c'.
    However, in practical situations it might be easier first to locate a specific hue 'ø' in the colour circle in terms of the proportion of chromatic attributes (75 per cent 'y' and 25 per cent 'r') and then to locate its position in the colour triangle in terms of the relationship of 's', 'w' and 'c' (10 per cent 'w' and 60 per cent 'c').

In the same way a 'peach' (1) might be described as mostly whitish, slightly yellowish-red; an ultramarine (2) as a slightly reddish, blue-blackish; a brown (3) as mostly blackish, yellow-red. These three colours will have the following notations and positions in the NCS model:

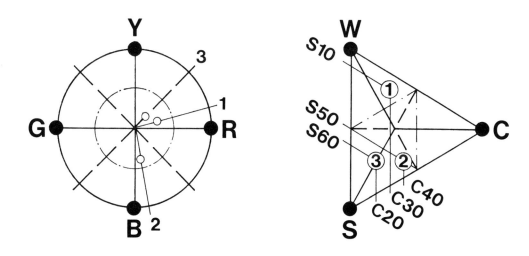

68
Notation of three colours in the NCS Circle and Triangle. (1) 1030 Y80R, (2) 5040 R90B, (3) 6020 Y50R. (For actual colour see figs. 93–5.)

Now let me remind you of the fact that the model is a graphical way of describing perceptual relationships between colours. In our model, the dots stand as symbols for colours and must not be confused with the actual perceptual phenomenon. Let us take an example.

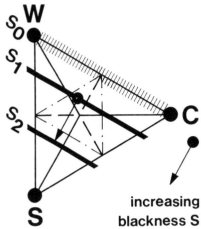

69

The meaning of equal blackness. By definition, pure white (w) and maximal colour (c) have no blackness. All other colours which, in common with (w) and (c), have no trace of blackness, will have their position within the colour triangle on the line (s_0) connecting (w) and (c).

These colours are often called 'bright'. Colours which are 'dull', 'dirty' or 'shadowed' and are perceptually more or less equal to black will, therefore, be positioned in the colour triangle nearer to black (s). If they are equally blackish, the dots will be marked on a straight line parallel to the w-c line as in s_1 and s_2. The latter dimensions represent two series of less (s_1), and more (s_2) equally blackish colour perceptions.

If the descriptive model is good and is a true representation of what is meant to be communicated, it is very practical when considering certain relationships. However, one is not meant to use the model as proof of the phenomenon it intends to describe. Figures 70–73 describe some perceptual colour phenomena with the aid of the NCS model.

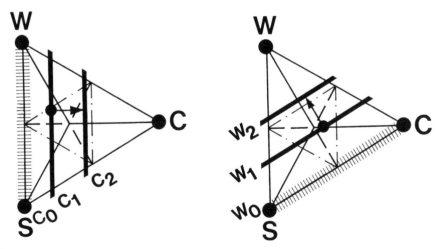

70 (*left:*)

The meaning of equal 'chromaticness'. On the w–s line we mark all colours which, in agreement with black and white, show no 'chromaticness'. These — colours with equal hue — will be positioned on lines parallel with the w–s axis as with c_1 and c_2.

71 (*right:*)

The meaning of equal whiteness. Colours without any perceptual whiteness are marked along the w_0 line. These are often called 'deep' colours, with increasing equal whiteness on lines w_1 and w_2.

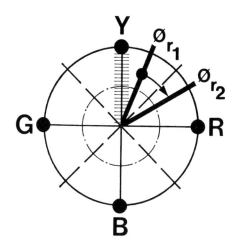 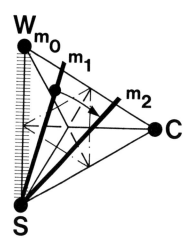

72 *(left:)*
The meaning of constant hue. Around the circumference are marked the colours of varying hue and along the radius are marked the colours of constant hue, i.e., colours with the same visual proportion of two chromatic attributes (e.g. yellowness–redness). The radius at Y means that one cannot trace any redness or greenness in the colours. Colours of two different proportions of redness are marked with straight lines as in ø and ø$_{r2}$. At ø$_{r1}$ the redness is about 25 per cent and at ø$_{r2}$, about 75 per cent.

73 *(right:)*
The meaning of saturation. Here we represent another type of constant proportion between two attributes. In the NCS it is called constant saturation (m) and is defined as: $m = \dfrac{c}{c+w}$ or $\dfrac{c}{100-s}$

This kind of perception is often called a 'shadow series', i.e. a chromatic coloured surface perceived in increasing depth of shadow (the word 'saturation' in English colour literature is often synonymous with what here we call 'chromaticness').

Experimental Documentation
I have presented the simple descriptive colour-perception model which is called the NCS, together with some constances in degree and proportion of the elementary colour attributes generated from this perceptual colour theory. This development towards a colour notation system has been approved as a Swedish standard for colour descriptions.

We have, at the Swedish Colour Centre Foundation, been deeply involved in experimental work aimed at discovering the degree to which people are capable of quantifying their colour perceptions in NCS terms. This was a research project to document the Hering theories and to formulate the metric of the NCS colour notation system which would prepare the way for an NCS colour atlas.

The results of more than 20,000 judgements have shown that it is possible to quantatively determine the degree of similarity to the six elementary colours. A number of subjects, with no knowledge of colour theories, were given the definitions of the six elementary colours. For example:

White: Your imagination of a pure white containing no trace of any 'chromaticness' (yellowness, redness, etc) or any blackness (or greyness).

Yellow: Your imagination of a pure yellow containing no trace of any greenness or redness and also no whiteness or blackness.

Following this instruction, they were then given various colour samples in a controlled viewing situation and asked to determine their similarity to the elementary colours in a figure 0-100, in such a way that the sum of the similarities (elementary colour attributes) add up to 100.

Our extensive experiments have resulted in the following findings:

(1) People are capable of making this type of judgement without any available physical references. It is probable that our colour perceptual systems contain some built-in references to which we relate all the colours we perceive. This is supported by more recent physiological research findings and can also be verified by Berlin and Kay who have shown that the first 'colour words' in different languages have emerged in the following order: white, black, red, yellow, green and blue (words for what have been called here the elementary colours).

(2) Under specific viewing conditions our colour samples are representative for their NCS notations. However, with normal variations in these conditions, they will still remain acceptable if we bear in mind that we always have to account with a certain variation around the mean-value in all types of psychophysical estimations.

(3) Generally, from our experiments one can conclude that, as we required no physical references for the judgements, it is possible to use the NCS colour descriptive method to specify the colour perception of certain stimuli in *any* situation comprising of: (1) the painted surface, (2) the actual light source, (3) the specific viewing condition (angle, distance, size), (4) the adaptation situation, (5) and possibly the difference in colour sense between observers, provided the words hold any meaning to them. Thus, the NCS determination method is valuable in all colour analyses of the environment.

There are many names for different colours but often they specifically relate to a meaning or a colour perception peculiar to an individual. 'Sky blue' might, for one individual, represent a whitish blue; for a second person it might represent a strong blue and, for a third, a deep blue. The use of one word for each colour perception is impossible and with the apparent difficulties in colour communication we need a descriptive but numerically based colour notation system. It should be adaptable to different levels of precision and workable without dependence upon colour samples or physical specifications. In other words, it must be based upon the assumption that the human being is the only true colour-measuring instrument. This is true for the NCS and, therefore, it can be said to be a reasonably good solution to the demand for a universal descriptive colour language.

The NCS Colour Atlas
I have stressed the fact that the NCS system requires no colour samples or physical specification of colour stimuli to describe colour perceptions. However, in many situations it is practical to have a number of systematically arranged colour samples. The NCS Colour Atlas would be advantageous and time-saving especially for educational purposes or in the study and communication of different colour

combinations. The Colour Atlas, comprising of approximately 1400 colour samples, will cover every tenth step within a range based on today's available pigments. It is possible to identify nearly 7,000 colours by visual interpolation between the systematically arranged samples in the Atlas. Under controlled viewing and illumination conditions, the physical radiation of NCS colours are also specified in the CIE (the Commission Internationale de l'Eclairage system of colorimetry).

A Comparison of the NCS with other Colour Systems
In the NCS one is working with one concept — that is, the degree of similarity of colours to the six imaginary references. In this respect the NCS can be said to be a clean system as it does not try to compromise a number of different colour concepts in one system. It shows the relationship in *'content'* of the six perceptual colour *'qualities'*: whiteness, blackness, yellowness, redness, blueness and greenness. These contents of the attributes of elementary colour are scaled metrically, giving a logical base for a colour notation. The scales are uniform with respect to the perceptual attributes involved. However, the primary aim of the NCS is not to demonstrate equal differences or discrimination between adjacent colours in the system, but to research the problem of colour contrast versus colour content.

From the NCS metrication, other parameters such as constant hue, saturation, brightness, greyness, deepness and brownness, can be explored and defined.

The Munsell system uses three parameters: hue, chroma and value which are, more or less, defined with references to the colour samples in the Munsell *Book of Colour*. In literature and scientific discussion it is often pleaded that the Munsell system shows equidistant differences between colour samples in each of the three parameters. However, at the same time, the system attempts to show some qualitative aspects of colour such as constant hue and constant chroma plus the physical aspect — constant value. Constant value is defined as constant luminous factor (reflected light) according to the CIE.

The artist, A. H. Munsell, originated the system and designed the first book of colour himself. In 1943 the colour samples were physically measured by a working group within the Optical Society of America. The measurements were evaluated in the CIE system, and the result was evened out with respect to the CIE parameters. However, to my knowledge, no experiments have shown either that the original colour selection was equidistant or quality based, or that it is possible to join the concept of equal difference (discrimination) with concepts of constant hue, chroma or value (quality).

Much contrary experimental evidence indicates that equidistance between adjacent colours is impossible to describe in a three-dimensional model, but would require at least seven or eight dimensions. However, there seems much in common between the NCS and the original Munsell system and more research and contact might result in a future synthesis of the two systems.

Another well-known colour system is the Ostwald model, exemplified in the *Colour Harmony Manual*. The Ostwald geometrical model is formally very similar to the NCS model. This, however, is a coincidence and is probably due to the fact that Hering presented the Natural Colour System forty-five years before the Ostwald system. In its current practice one can detect an obvious confusion between basic perceptual concepts and physical, optical or chemical colour stimulus mixing. In its practical application, this system used to represent maximum chromatic colour (full colour) with the most chromatic pigment for each hue. Also, contrary to the NCS, corresponding points in the colour triangle for different hues do not represent colours of equal *visual* 'chromaticness' but an equal mixture of the full colour with white and/or black pigments.

The Universal Application of the NCS in Environmental Design Studies
In the NCS one characterizes colours from the point of view of 'quality' and this is
possible without any physical colour sample references. This means that we can
describe perceived colours in arbitrary situations and, thus, we can study colour and
colour combinations in the environment without the need to relate to a specific
physical relationship. If we need to establish this relationship then, of course, we
have to specify the specific conditions.

This method has been used to study the loss of visual information in colour
television signal, from the studio situation to the consumer's own receiver. Colour
situations in landscape and townscape have also been analysed in order to
understand more about the role of colour in specific spaces. In these types of
environmental colour analyses it was found practical to use the NCS graphical model
for notations.

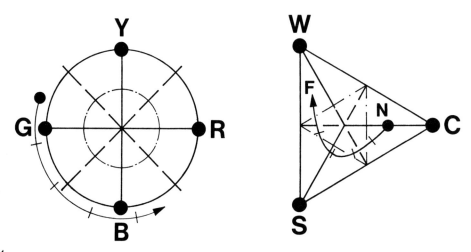

74
Variation of tree foliage colour with distance. Only hue is marked in the colour circle; relationships
between whiteness, blackness and 'chromaticness' are marked in the colour triangle.

The illustration below is an example of the colour analysis of tree foliage perceived
at different distances from near (N), where one could see the colour of the leaves, to
very far (F) — when the colour of the forest is only a small part of the total landscape.
From a fairly strong yellowish green the colour initially becomes deeper — a more
blackish green — and gradually bluish green but with decreasing 'chromaticness'.
At a distance of approximately one mile, the colour slowly becomes whitish grey and
ends up as a reddish blue at about ten miles distant.

A look into the future will expose the need for more knowledge about colour as a
means of creating a better world for human beings. We at the Swedish Colour Centre
are concentrating our efforts in studying: (1) colour perceptions of specified colour
surfaces under various viewing conditions, distance, light, surface structure, etc. (2)
further psychological relationships related to the NCS model, (3) a theory of colour
combinations.

The aim of the above research project is to fill the gap in information concerning
the behaviour of colour in different situations. Most specialists within environmental design obtain their information by a process of trial and error. We also need to
know if there is something which could be called 'visual pollution' and, if it exists,
whether it is possible to avoid it. We hope to be able to offer these results in the form
of a handbook when we have covered the field.

If we really want to deal with these types of problem — which are already topical

— we must understand more about colour perception and the continuing psychological responses. We must increase our knowledge of the perceptual or subjective colour qualities in order to learn more about the use of architectural colour and, hopefully, a more humane future environment. It is not enough to study colour as a physical phenomenon in order to produce coloured materials because first of all we need a colour language which will communicate our experiences, findings and thoughts (figs. 92–7).

Interior Space and Colour

Prof. Carl-Axel Acking and Dr Rikard Küller

How does colour influence the appearance of a room? and has it any profound influence upon those people who experience the space? Questions such as these are certainly not new — Goethe asked them as did Leonardo before him. Many speculative or scientifically based answers have been proposed but the body of knowledge is insubstantial — many of the answers being either obvious or dubious.

In a series of experiments we have tried to contribute to the understanding of architectural and psychological problems related to colour. As many of the earlier investigations used coloured samples as stimuli we thought it important to judge colour, not as isolated patches, but as part of the environment either in the form of drawings or in real situations. We began with drawings and later carried out validation studies in full-scale rooms which, in general, supported the initial studies.

75
Perspective drawing used in the Acking and Küller experiment.

A typical drawing room was chosen and a perspective drawing made. The effects of colours on the room were then systematically investigated by asking people to judge the perspective in which the colour of the walls and some of the furniture and fittings were varied and presented in eighty-nine different colour combinations. The main result of this study, as based on our earlier factor analytical experiments of environmental dimensions of perception, can be summarized as follows:
(1) Positive correlation $(r=.76)$ between lightness and judged openness.
(2) Positive correlation $(r=.81)$ between 'chromaticness' and judged complexity.
(3) Positive correlation $(r=.72)$ between blackness and social evaluation.
(4) Positive correlation $(r=.65)$ between blackness and judged potency.
(5) Lack of general results from the evaluation of the 'pleasantness factor'. We will discuss these results in more detail.

The apparent spaciousness and openness of room spaces are influenced by many factors such as the shape of the room, the number, size and shape of windows, the characteristics of artificial light, the furniture and the lightness of the walls, ceiling and floor planes. It is quite clear, however, that lightness is one of the most important factors and that it is easy to control and easy to change. In our test, perceived 'openness' or spaciousness increased as lightness increased in either the interior details or the walls. The correlations between judged openness and lightness of walls was high $(r=.76)$. Spaciousness also increased with a corresponding increase in the

120

chromatic strength of interior details but no such dependence was noted when chromatic strength was increased in the walls. When the chromatic strength of details increased, the contrast between the details and walls was naturally enhanced. It might be this contrast effect and not the higher chromatic strength in itself that resulted in judgements of higher openness.

Lightness also influences room shape. Rarely will one find a room in which all the surfaces are of equal lightness and often the ceiling is off-white or white while the floor plane is considerably darker with lightness levels of walls located somewhere between the two. There are practical and aesthetic reasons for this as, for example, if all the surfaces were similar in lightness the room might be felt to lack character. In order to introduce character the relative lightness of walls is often varied. The influence of lightness on shape might be formulated thus: dark surfaces attract each other, while light surfaces repel each other. Accordingly, a dark ceiling will cause that plane to appear lower; two dark and two light walls in opposition will make the room appear short one way and long the other.

If knowledge such as this is to be applied, for example, to change the appearance of a room shape, the general illumination should be considered. The wall plane opposite the window should generally be kept fairly light or it will absorb much of the daylight and make for uneven illumination. The window wall should also be light together with the windowsill and frame so that the contrast with the sky is not too great; a contrast which could cause irritating glare and even headaches. To conclude, it must be kept in mind that colour lightness (more clearly expressed as 'whiteness' and 'blackness') is something different from illumination but in practice the two should always be considered together.

If lightness is important for the appearance of room spaciousness and shape, colour strength is as important for 'complexity'. Weak colours give a room an impression of calmness, strong colours make it appear exciting. In our study we found a high, positive correlation $(r=.81)$ with perceived complexity which means that complexity increased as chromatic strength increased but no such dependence was found on lightness. Generally speaking, a strong green was found to be as exciting as a strong red. This is interesting because some writers have reported considerable differences in the physiological influences of these two colours. When Kurt Goldstein dressed his experimental subject (who had a serious balance defect) in a green frock she appeared to walk quite normally, but when dressed in red she could hardly walk at all and was in constant danger of falling. This and other differences in the reported effects of green and red are as yet unexplained but might have little to do with how exciting a colour appears.

It seems evident that not only colour strength but also colour contrast contributes to the impression of complexity in a room. Many different and strong colours will be of importance here as will the duration of room experience. Does a short time spent in a theatre or restaurant where strong colours are used on walls, curtains and carpets give rise to a festive and active attitude, while the effect of the same colours might be tiresome during a prolonged stay in hospital? Would a person, as Goethe claimed, become weakminded if he spent considerable time in a room with violet walls? Until now, no general formulation has been established which includes these factors.

Apart from the findings for lightness and colour strength, there are some others worth mentioning. 'Blackness', as defined by the NCS, seems quite straightforwardly related to an expression of 'potency' and 'social status'; dark coloured rooms appearing to be considered more expensive and potent. The correlation figures for one room amounted to $r=.72$ for social status and $r=.65$ for potency. Why people should associate dark hues with concepts of expensiveness and potency is not known although there might be a cultural influence. However, a comparative study conducted by Lars Sivik in Sweden and Greece does not seem to warrant this conclusion.

Concerning colour preference Eysenck's 'universal scale' may be valid in a very general way but as he was unable to specify either lightness or colour strength, and as the stimulus material consisted of mainly coloured sheets of paper, the result is of no practical consequence when applied to the colouring of interiors. In our investigations we have taken great care in attempting to establish general relationships between colour dimensions and perceived 'pleasantness' of interiors but have, hitherto, found no simple dependence either upon colour strength, lightness or hue. As a matter of fact, we found no evidence whatsoever of any general hue preference order. The differences we detected within hues were, as a rule, far greater than the differences in preference between the various hues. The reason why a specific colour patch might be generally agreed to be more pleasant than another at present eludes description.

It seems, in conclusion, that there are systematic relationships between some dimensions of colour on the one hand and some general perceptual dimensions on the other. The relationships concerning spatial enclosedness and complexity are fairly simple, but those concerning the evaluation of pleasantness are more complicated. It is also interesting to note that fairly simple experiments with drawings and colour slides have a fair amount of predictive power; this should, however, be no excuse for omitting full-scale studies.

During the last few years there has been an increasing interest in environmental factors, many of which have been shown beyond doubt to have a profound and often adverse effect on man. Has colour such an effect? Some investigations suggest, for example, that the coloration of nursery schools might influence the development of intelligence and the personality traits of children. Until now these claims have not been substantiated but the issue is of such importance that it demands a thorough investigation. Without doubt, colour seems as open to speculation today as it has ever been. As Goethe put it, 'If you hold a red cloth before a bull he will get furious, but if you as much as hint at colour the philosopher will go frantic'!

122

The Language of Colour: Colour Connotations

Dr Lars Sivik

Most people think that colours make them feel happy. If this is true, it may be also valid the other way round. If we are happy we see everything in colour — 'we want to paint the world'. The opposite of colour in this context is lack of colour — greyness; a concept associated in most languages with boredom and sadness.

Associations and attitudes to colours are, like all evaluations, subjective — unique for the individual. They depend upon the situation and vary over time. Attitudes to colour probably originate to a great degree from early learning processes and, thus, have a cultural basis. One can well imagine that our inherent ability to see colours may also be connected with our emotions; there is certainly evidence of affinity between perception and 'emotional' behaviour among other species.

The relatively high agreement between people about colour meaning might be mainly due to the fact that colour serves as information about our surrounding world. By looking through a window we can see from colour nuances what kind of weather it is; a banana is yellow when it is ripe and fresh, not green or brown. The connection between colour and moods, affections and associations, has always been seen as something concrete, something we ought to be able to study.

It would be valuable to know how similarly we experience the different colour stimuli, and also if we generally agree with those who, in creating our milieu, apply colours to the objects which surround us. If, as a basis for making decisions, we can achieve information which might improve on mere guesswork, then we are undoubtedly making progress. The first experimental psychologists questioned whether or not there is a specific preference order among different colours. However, the outcome of these investigations is of limited value because of the lack of control of both the stimulus material and the conditions of light and observation.

A person with normal colour vision can distinguish between thousands of colours all of which can be named as 'red'. Which one of these is found to be exciting? It is often said that green is calming. Which green, viridian, emerald or grass green?

It seems that many of the investigators of colour connotations had little knowledge of colour systems while the colour metricians were little interested in colour connotations. These were the basic reasons for carrying out a study of colour meaning as part of the research programme at the Swedish Colour Centre. The starting point was the Natural Colour System.

Our intention was to study people's attitudes to and associations with individual colours, in an awareness that one colour seldom appears alone and in isolation from a context. However, we have to begin somewhere.

We have many stereotyped ideas about colour: red is active, orange is warm. Artists in particular hold many fixed conceptions concerning the psychological 'attributes' of colour. Does everyone share these ideas? Are there any systematic differences of meaning between different colour areas and, if so, would it be possible to map them?

Seventy colour samples were judged one by one against the so-called semantic differential scales by a large number of subjects under standardized conditions. The results unambiguously illustrated sufficient agreement between people to establish different averages from a subject group for different colours. For most scales of meaning the averages changed systematically while moving from one colour region to another. For example, the scale of old-young co-varied with the dimensions of blackness. This means that the more a colour darkens, the more it is associated with the concept of 'old'.

The relationship between colour meaning and colour appearance is mostly non-linear and quite complex but it can be illustrated in the following way. If a colour is defined according to the NCS system it occupies a fixed position in the colour space. In the graphic model it can be marked by a point on the hue circle and a point within the colour triangle. The seventy colours were, in this way, defined as geographical points in the colour world model and, with defined values for their various meanings, we were able to draw a 'weather chart' much in the same way as the meteorologist connects points of equal temperature on a map. In our colour maps (the colour triangles) we connect the colours that have the same value or meaning and we call the lines 'isosemantic', i.e., lines of equal meaning. The reader will be, of course, familiar with other colour solids and triangles such as those used in the Munsell and Ostwald systems; the procedure of drawing isosemantic lines can naturally be applied to any three-dimensional colour space.

In our study, where isolated colour patches were judged, twenty-six scales of meaning were used. The isosemantic patterns for one of the scales — tranquillizing-exciting — is shown below.

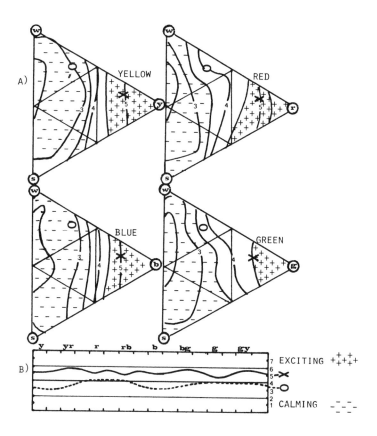

76
The four triangles represent the hues of yellow, red, blue and green respectively and the lower diagram shows the variation of meaning over the different hues when whiteness, blackness and chromatic strength are held constant. The isosemantic map patterns can be read in the following way. First, we can see that the four triangles appear very similar; it is not the hue but the strength of the colour — its level of saturation—that is crucial when the colour is perceived as calming or exciting. As it can be seen, the most tranquillizing are those colours along the grey axis; the more the colour strength is increased, the more the colour represents the variation between the different hues at a certain 'chromaticness', whiteness and blackness — namely the position marked by the cross in the triangles. The dotted line, a ring in the triangles, represents a hue circle that consists of pale pastel colours which are judged to be quite neutral or slightly tranquillizing; while the strong ones were all on the exciting side, regardless of hue.

124

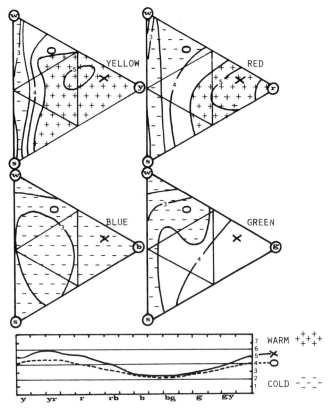

77
As can be seen, both the colour of the hue and its position in the triangle are important in the warm–cold association, i.e. the colour strength and its whiteness and blackness. The warmest colours are those from yellow to red provided they are quite strong, with a maximum warmth in orange. All blue colours, regardless of strength and other qualities, are colder. The area of warmth returns when we move towards green and back to yellow.

Now let us examine an example where the hue *is* of importance — the well-known synaesthesia of colour and temperature. The sensation of warmth is not originally perceived by the eye but yet we find it natural to talk of warm and cold colours (fig. 77).

The values of the different colours for the twenty-six scales were studied by factor analysis and it was found that they could be represented by four factors or dimensions of meaning: one factor, which we called the *excitement factor,* co-varied with colour strength (fig. 78). Another factor was called the *evaluation factor* — this is a kind of preference ordering of the various colours and contains scales such as 'positive-negative', 'beautiful-ugly', 'tasteful-distasteful'. A third factor we called *potency factor* because it consisted of variables such as 'energetic', 'masculine' and 'secure'. This factor showed a considerable co-variation with the colour dimension of blackness, the fourth dimension was the *temperature factor* already mentioned.

Perhaps the most conspicuous conclusion was that the colour dimensions of hue had such a small impact on most of the semantic scales, whereas it was very critical whether a colour was weak or strong in saturation, blackness or whiteness. The exception was, however, the 'warm-cold' and related scales. The proverbial phrase that green colours, in general, have a calming effect is thus strongly questioned. Furthermore, people do not consider red to be more active than any other hue, of colours of equal strength, blackness and whiteness are compared.

It should be mentioned that the investigation was also carried out in Greece in

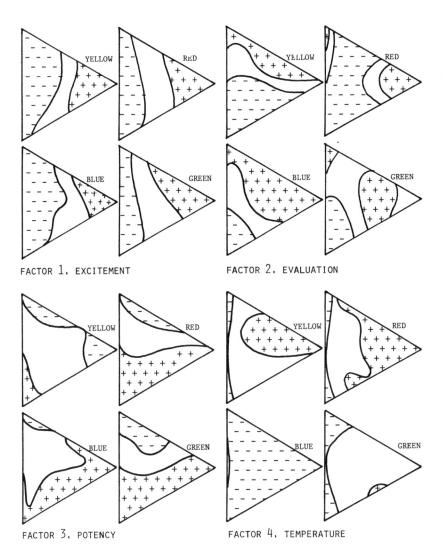

FACTOR 1. EXCITEMENT

FACTOR 2. EVALUATION

FACTOR 3. POTENCY

FACTOR 4. TEMPERATURE

78

Excitement factor. Evaluation factor. Potency factor. Temperature factor. The above diagrams are further simplified by the marking of the different zones. The colour zone with plus signs indicates colours which have high values for the actual factor of meaning; the white zone is neutral, containing those colours that are neither positive or negative in the factor. Negative zones, marked with minus signs, indicate colours with significantly negative values in this dimension of meaning.

order to study possible cultural differences. Some differences were found, but were not great. For basic concepts such as 'hilarious–serious', 'like–dislike', 'old–young' there were no significant differences between Greeks and Swedes. Deviations did show up for other variables reflecting different frames of reference, for example, 'winter–summer'. Northern people associate light blue and greens with winter (ice and snow) and this, of course, was not the case for Athenians. Concepts relating to masculine and feminine colours did not differ concerning the systematic variation along the colour dimensions (increased blackness=increased manliness). However, the Greek results were displaced as all colours were judged to be more feminine than in the Swedish test. This is compatible with the fact that in Greece men do not wear highly coloured clothes.

This study succeeded in demonstrating that it is feasible to map general attitudes and connotations to colour through the use of scientific methods and a reliable colour system. In this experiment the subjects were randomly sampled and the colour samples judged one by one in neutral surroundings. The variations between the individuals were much smaller than the variation caused by the deviation in colour, but sufficiently great to provoke the question of whether or not the inter-individual differences are systematic.

The experiments thus far were concerned only with the meaning of colours as such. Rectangular colour samples were judged in isolation from other colours. What pattern of colour meaning would emerge if the colours were viewed in the context of particular objects? Provided we can control all the conditions and produce the proper stimuli, it is possible to investigate this. However, if variations occurred in form, colour and context, it would be difficult to detect the cause of any variation in meaning.

Connotations to Exterior Colours on Buildings

In the face of all the difficulties, we attempted to map colour meanings in a particular context. We used the same attitude instrument and the same number of stimulus colours as in the previous test. We were not able to colour real buildings but, with a

79, 80
The two types of building used in the experiment, the 'high house', (*top*) and the 'low house' (*overleaf*).

127

special technique of photo-simulation, the façades' colours were varied on colour prints. Two pictures were used and called 'high house' and 'low house'. The former was a photograph of a three-storey multifamily house and the latter, an ordinary one-storey chain house common in Sweden.

We set out to answer the following questions: What are the relationships between colour meaning and colour appearance when colours are a part of a building? Would resultant isosemantic patterns deviate from those in our former investigation? How concordant are the subjects in this case? Would there be any systematic differences in attitudes to the coloration between the two types of buildings used in the test?

Some aspects of the results can be mentioned here. The semantic scales or word pairs used were selected from earlier factor analysis studies related to general architectural concepts and they formed the following groups of factors (pp.130–31):

81, 82, 83
These three photographs demonstrate transformations in model form of an interior space articulated with coloured planes. It is illuminated with white, blue, and green light respectively. These experiments with coloured illumination are projects by students in Professor Preusser's Environmental Light and Colour course in the Department of Architecture at the Massachussetts Institute of Technology.

81

82

83

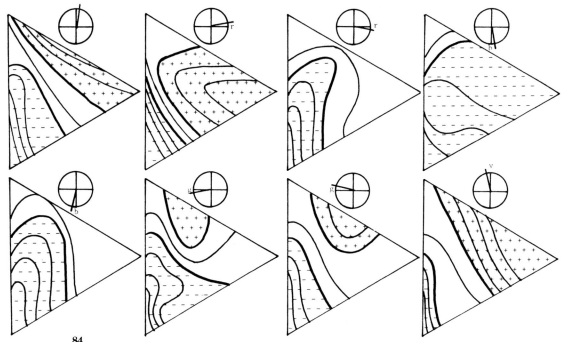

84

Emotional evaluation (pleasantness). The maps opposite for the 'high house' are based on factor scores. This factor, derived from scales such as beautiful–ugly, friendly–hostile, etc. can be interpreted as a preference order of the colours in this context. In this factor of meaning, the largest deviations from the previous study were found. In connection with the hue dimension, the preferences reflect the common architectural colours found in Sweden. The yellow–red sector with the area between green and yellow is familiar. However, we discovered a positive response to far stronger colours than those usually seen in the environment. The opposite hue area — those between red and blue and between blue and green — are liked somewhat less except for the lightest colours. Pure grey and greyish buildings always achieved the lowest response and black the least.

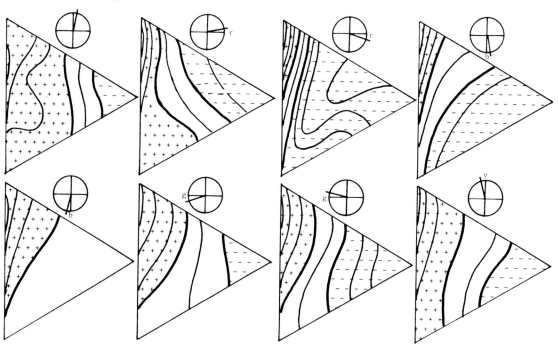

85

Factor two consisted of scales such as vulgar–cultured, calming–exciting, unusual–common, and corresponds to the excitement factor in the last study. A clear co-variation with dimension of colour strength.

130

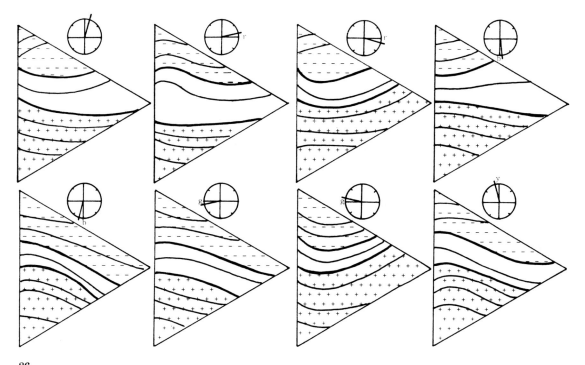

86

The third cluster of scales was easily identified as the spatial factor: open–closed, spacious–narrow, etc. The variance in this semantic variable, caused by changes in the house colours, seemed to depend almost entirely upon the blackness of a colour. The blacker or darker the house, the more enclosed is perceived the space between the buildings in the photographs. Hue has no impact at all. It was noticeable that these subtle changes in the experience of space can be caused by colour changes on the same house and these changes can be manifested as systematic differences in the group averages.

Could results such as these be applied to the planning of the real environment? Certainly not directly, for in the environment there are many factors which were not present in the investigation. However, anyone concerned with colour in the design of our environment should be interested in all new knowledge about the colour experience and in methods of adding to that knowledge.

It was suggested, as a spin-off from our study, that many of the conventions concerning colour concepts are wrong. For example, green is no more calming than red, provided that we compare colours of equal colour strength and blackness. There are many other conventional colour concepts which ought to be questioned. That one cannot predict the level of colour strength on a wall by looking at a small colour sample is something that every colour expert knows; the experienced colour is said to be stronger when applied to a larger area. This is not true. Repeated experiments have shown that small colour samples of five centimetres square are not judged weaker than the same colour perceived at a size of two metres square. On the other hand, one may experience a strongly coloured wall which induces an overwhelming impact, but this is something quite different — another psychological dimension, perhaps.

Another common stereotype is that we must avoid strong colours in our immediate surroundings. We are advised that we may 'tire of them in the long run', we may experience headaches or go mad as a result, and so on. Has anyone investigated this? It is most probable that we would adjust to the colours and, after a time, accept them without question. I mention these examples to demonstrate that we know far less than we believe about colour experiences and their implications.

In some larger Swedish towns, the use of architectural colour is increasing. It is mostly the older houses which are repainted with colour strengths which would have been unthinkable ten years ago. The reasons for the growing interest in

87

Skylab I-G Trainer Crew Quarters — clockwise from top: experiment work area, ward room, waste management, sleep compartment. Use of short wavelength colours to induce 'increased' space and long wavelength colours to indicate important objects. (Photo: Bain)

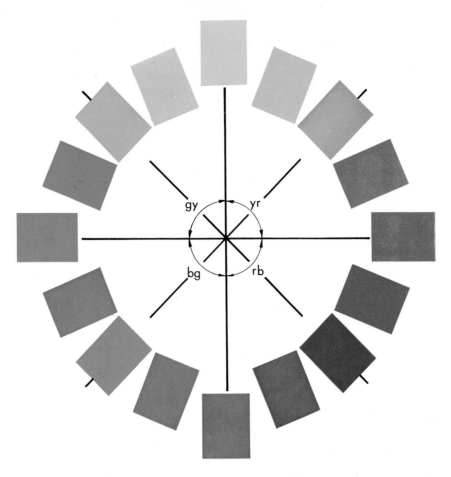

88 An NCS colour circle showing colour samples with variation in hue.

89 An NCS colour triangle showing twenty-four samples of the green hue located and responding to white, black and the maximal colour.

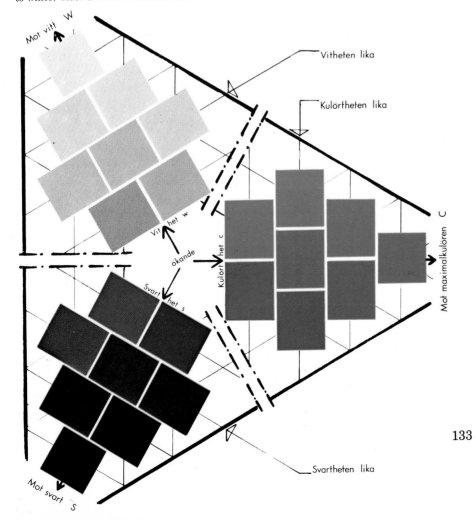

133

environmental colour are difficult to trace but one reason might be a counter-reaction from the grey suburbs. The appraisal of the new colour patches in the city landscape is mixed, particularly by those who are familiar with culture, history and architecture. Their opinions often differ from the thinking of the general populace, and they are also concerned when the 'wrong' colours are applied to old buildings. Accidental deviations from the proper style, however, do not seem to upset those who are unfamiliar with art history. The great majority of people are very positive to 'happier' colours in the townscape and are extremely critical of lack of colour.

Conclusions such as these can be drawn from a further series of investigations conducted at the University of Göteborg in the Department of Psychology. Altogether, more than six hundred people were interviewed in areas containing strongly coloured buildings and in areas of grey housing. Almost 100 per cent of those living in the coloured houses were happy to have colour in their environment and those few who, living in the grey area, did not dislike the external appearance of their dwellings did not, in fact, know what colour their houses were! The others used adjectives such as 'concrete boxes', 'bunkers', and the like, to describe their homes.

In a second study we evaluated people's attitudes to the colour restoration of the eighteenth-century buildings of Maria Östra in the old part of Stockholm. From the interviews it was possible to estimate how the answers might agree with the preference values predicted by the isosemantic maps:

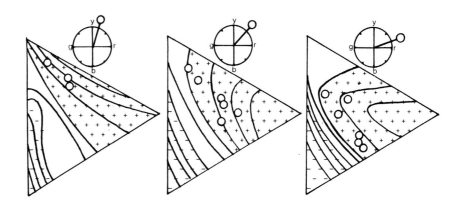

90
The three isosemantic maps represent the evaluation factor in the exterior study. The actual colours of the restored buildings are marked by rings within the diagrams. They all fall within the area of colours which are highly evaluated and, thus, the responses to our interviews accord well with the results of the laboratory study.

A further, similar enquiry was also carried out in Göteborg which elicited residents' attitudes to the colour of their buildings. Five areas were selected, each consisting of a number of similar buildings:

(A) The so-called 'Blue Town' consists of apartment blocks of five to nine storeys, all of an extraordinary strong blue.

(B) The second area contains three-storey red brick buildings with green roofs and blue balconies.

(C) The third area contains about fifty houses built mainly of wood, with gables painted in various pastel colours, none of which exceeds a 'chromaticness' of 30 per cent.

(D) The fourth area comprises of three-storey brownish grey buildings.

(E) The last area consists of eight-storey grey apartment blocks.

One hundred and thirty-six subjects were interviewed in their homes, and the central question asked was: How do you like the exterior colour of this building? As in previous studies, seven answers from 'very beautiful' through 'neither beautiful nor ugly' to 'very ugly' were offered as alternatives:

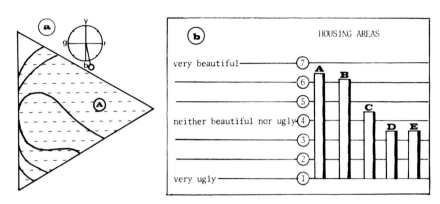

91
On the left is the isosemantic map showing the actual hue section of the blue building in area (A) as it was perceived and recorded on a sunny day. The colours in area (B) are varied in hue but all were within the neutral or positive zones in the isosemantic charts for the evaluative factor. The inhabitants of the grey areas (D and E) evaluated the coloration of their building lower than other subjects in the tests; a result which compares favourably with the laboratory findings.

The results from the blue area do not accord with the laboratory findings. The residents really loved the prevailing blue colour of their apartment blocks, when the same colour was intensely disliked in the laboratory. One reason may be that people quickly adjust to what at first appears to be an unusual and even disliked coloration. None of the subjects had chosen to live in the blue area, having moved there during a period of acute housing shortage.

The fact that the blue area residents had become familiar with the initially strange housing colour is possibly explained by some answers to questions put to residents in other areas in our study. People in area (B) — from which the blue buildings were visible — were also positive towards the blue colour, but not to the extent of the actual blue building residents. Residents in the other areas, who had only heard of the blue housing or had seen it in photographs, disliked the mere idea of living in a blue-painted, metal-clad apartment block!

Yet another set of interviews elicited a large number of attitude variables which support the findings of our laboratory studies. The subjects resided in four areas of Örebro in buildings discreetly and conventionally painted in colours within the neutral zones of the evaluation factor of the laboratory study. The residents' attitudes proved to be as neutral as the exterior colours, except that the residents of an area where some houses were painted in a pale violet. They considered this colour ugly, and had evidently not adjusted to it, even after several years. In conclusion, it may be suggested that these results, obtained from an interaction with real buildings, considerably validate the simulated laboratory study.

These investigations support the following theoretical propositions concerning the connotations of colour:

(1) A large number of studies indicate that many semantic variables (scales of meaning) generally remain stable over time and space when associated with isolated colour samples. For example, blue is the most preferred colour, yellow-red is the warmest, black the most serious, etc., and that this is valid for colour *per se*.

92
NCS notation — 1060 Y25R

93
NCS notation — 1030 Y80R

94
NCS notation — 5040 R90B

95
NCS notation — 6020 Y50R

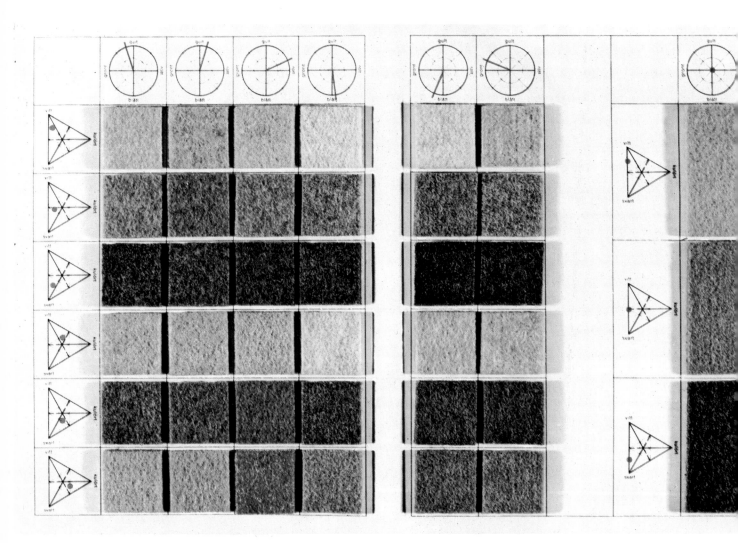

96
An application of NCS principles to industry. Anders Härd achieved maximum variety in his selection of a small range of colours for soft floor coverings.

136

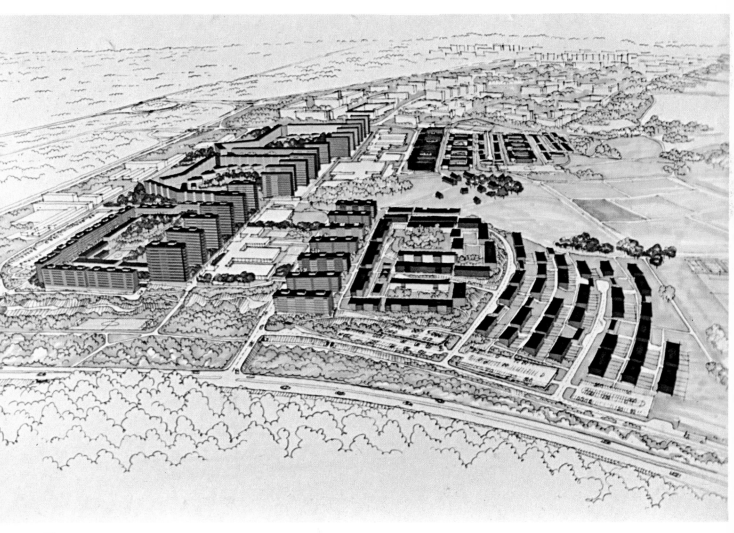

97
Environmental colour planning using scales from the NCS.

(2) By contrast, when colour is experienced as the coloration of an object or in a particular context the patterns of its connotations change *for some, but not for all, variables of meaning*. For example, blue is highly evaluated, even when on such a special evaluation scale as 'appetizing-unappetizing'. The meaning of blue, in this case, is a function of the intrinsic attributes of an object or context.

(3) Colours are more or less appropriate to a given object: natural objects can change colour within limits, and people, generally, are well aware if these limits are exceeded (compare reactions to a blue apple with those to a blue plum). However, we are also justified in talking about object colours which have become accepted by a process of cultural conditioning. Strong blue or pale violet buildings are most unusual in Sweden, and Swedes, therefore, react negatively when they first experience them.

(4) People can adjust to particular colours, but only in certain circumstances: (a) If the colour is naturally or culturally appropriate to the object. Cars, pencils or books, for example, are not expected to be of any particular colour and people will, therefore, come to accept them in a wide range of hues. (b) If the colour, as such, is liked. People do adjust to unusual house colours if they do not basically dislike the colour as such. This was the case in the blue area, and a point raised spontaneously by many subjects during the interviews. The residents in that part of the housing area which contained some pale violet and grey buildings could not bring themselves to stomach these colours, a finding in agreement with the laboratory studies which also revealed that pale violet and grey are strongly disliked.

(5) We have suggested that the patterns of connotations for certain variables of meaning, in particular the evaluative ones, depend largely on the context in which the colours appear. Other variables, on the other hand, are perceived to have very little relevance to the object and, therefore, serve only to describe or characterize the colour as such. Returning to the blue apple, the concepts of warmth are irrelevant to the apple but not to the colour. Blue is generally perceived as cold, regardless of whether or not it is the coloration of an apple, a piece of paper, or the wall of a building. The corollary may be true when attributes of the object influence attitudes to its colour. Which, for example, appears the warmer, an ice-blue woollen sock or a red plastic bag? Such circumstances may cause a conflict of feeling, and to resolve it one is forced to distinguish between the object and its colour — something that is rarely done. In some way, all the variables of meaning can be analysed for the varying relevance to the colour or to the object or to the synthesis of or interaction between the two.

From the interview questions, common to many of our investigations carried out in relation to the urban environment, it can be concluded that *people consider it self-evident that colour is an important factor in environmental design*. People also think that one is made happier by 'happy' environmental colours and sad by dull environmental colours. It is notable that the majority of subjects express a very low estimation of the taste and reliability of those who, in reality, make decisions concerning the creation of the environment. They also believe that a greater freedom would allow them, as individuals, to create and design according to their taste.

In Sweden, stringent restrictions concerning the use of external environment colours have existed for many years — unity and discretion having been the time-honoured concepts. The decision-making authorities are probably educated in both culture and art history but they have little knowledge of the preferences of the vast majority of people; mainly because such knowledge has never been sought.

138

The greyness of our new suburbs, however, cannot be entirely blamed on our community architects. There has been an acute housing shortage and large construction companies have decided on the cheapest for the short term with little consideration for aesthetic values.

If I have conveyed the impression that a wider and strong use of environmental colour will make everyone happier, then I have expressed myself badly. Colour is one of the many factors in the design of the built environment but it demands study and should be considered from the onset of any environmental design programme. As a rule, it proves unsuccessful to attempt to conceal dull and monotonous architecture with strong colours. It is also pathetic when, in an era of system-building, we have to use colour as a cue for people to find their way home.

The concept of values has been mentioned. What is beautiful and what is ugly? One criterion on which a choice could be made is that as many people as possible should be content. This choice, of course, also implies values.

HEAVY
LIGHT

DEFINED
UNDEFINED

CLOSED
OPEN

MASCULINE
FEMININE

UNUSUAL
COMMON

EXCITING
CALMING

HILARIOUS
SERIOUS

CULTURED
VULGAR

BEAUTIFUL
UGLY

PLEASANT
UNPLEASANT

FRIENDLY
UNFRIENDLY

WARM
COLD

HEAVY
LIGHT

DEFINED
UNDEFINED

CLOSED
OPEN

MASCULINE
FEMININE

UNUSUAL
COMMON

EXCITING
CALMING

HILARIOUS
SERIOUS

CULTURED
VULGAR

BEAUTIFUL
UGLY

PLEASANT
UNPLEASANT

FRIENDLY
UNFRIENDLY

WARM
COLD

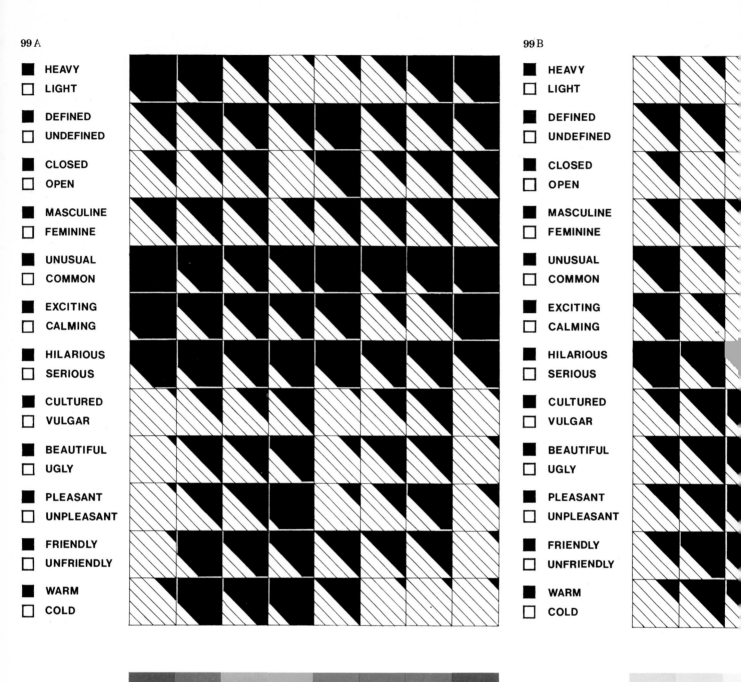

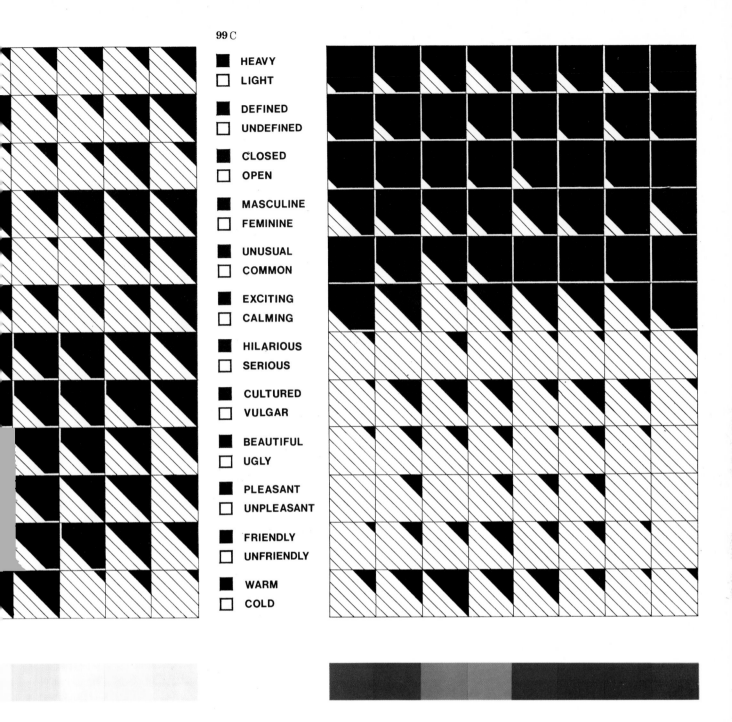

■	HEAVY
□	LIGHT
■	DEFINED
□	UNDEFINED
■	CLOSED
□	OPEN
■	MASCULINE
□	FEMININE
■	UNUSUAL
□	COMMON
■	EXCITING
□	CALMING
■	HILARIOUS
□	SERIOUS
■	CULTURED
□	VULGAR
■	BEAUTIFUL
□	UGLY
■	PLEASANT
□	UNPLEASANT
■	FRIENDLY
□	UNFRIENDLY
■	WARM
□	COLD

141

Towards the Meaning of Environmental Colour

In the diagram on pp.140–41 we have attempted to plot the meanings we associate with particular colours when judged in an architectural context. This is based, in the main, on the findings and validations of Lars Sivik and it must be stated that colour meanings in this display relate only to the hues, tints and shades illustrated. However, it does present the designer with some indication of the connotative meaning of colour which might be considered and incorporated into the building design.

The diagram is easy to read; the amount of agreement is denoted by the proportions of black and white. For example, a gradually descending scale for the warm–cold dimension reads as follows:

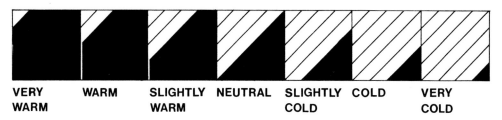

| VERY WARM | WARM | SLIGHTLY WARM | NEUTRAL | SLIGHTLY COLD | COLD | VERY COLD |

As further research and validation studies become available this kind of information could become more comprehensive, include colour combinations, and act in a more predictive role. We might also learn which scales of meaning are affected by time and taste (although there is considerable agreement that some colour meanings hold good over time and across cultures) together with colour interactions with diverse space, texture, size and shape.

However, if the study of colour in the spatial experience is more elusive than one would wish at this point in time we have, until further information becomes available, to make more indirect inferences from the existing data.

The ultimate reason for any scientific study of colour is to learn how to utilize it so as to have a predictable effect on people, and before the designer can begin to apply any information he must initially define criteria against which the effect of a specific environment should be established. In other words, he should predetermine how a person might feel or react within a particular space and then develop colour relationships at an early stage in relation to spatial function or the tasks which may be performed within it. This approach could contribute important knowledge to our understanding of colour–space interaction if followed up by observational or experimental studies in the completed environment.

An interplay of colour along the dimensions of hue, saturation and brightness, and along the synaesthetic scales of warm–cold, near–far, big–small and light–heavy can be articulated in controlling, to an extent, the character and feeling of architectural space. A knowledge of colour phenomena can also assist the designer and be employed in intensifying the spatial experience. For example, if complementary colours are perceived alternately in a spatial sequence, such as in linked rooms or corridors, the resulting negative after-image induced by one space will visually reinforce the colour impression made by the next.

Environmentally, colour can be manipulated to increase or decrease the apparent spatial dimensions through a conscious articulation of colour wavelength, colour contrast and figure–ground relationships; the distance and size of planes and objects being basically regulated by the brightness level of surface pigment. Using the findings from the majority of colour preference investigations as a broad frame of reference, the built environment could, with the availability of synthetic materials, safely accommodate a much wider use of the wealth of colours which emanate from the blue and green region of the spectrum — especially in the external environment.

In large-scale or more complex situations, the designer can employ the apparent weight of colour to establish stability in both internal and external environments. The 'heavy' colours — saturated reds, blues and violets — could be articulated to encourage equilibrium in spaces where a positive gravitational link between floor and ceiling plane is important. The possibilities of this synaesthetic relationship could also be applied to other component elements of space. For example, if a red mass is supported by a yellow column, it could be perceived as appearing less stable than if the colours were reversed. Externally, colour-weight synaesthesia could be manipulated in the form of ascending horizontal gradations on the façades of high-rise buildings or skyscrapers with the 'heaviest' colour at their base. In this fashion they could be 'fixed' in space with a colour anchor, the base colour creating a stronger relationship with the human scale and the colour gradations providing some identification with areas of the building. Conversely, the 'lightweight' colours — yellows and greens — could reduce the apparent heaviness of dominant and overpowering architectural mass.

Together with apparent depth, the effects of colour on apparent temperature have also been widely used by interior designers and there has been considerable reporting of the now classic instances of waiting-rooms and toilets which, after complaints by users and without the addition of any heating installation, generate illusions of warmth as a result of the simple application of red paint. A fully saturated red is generally accepted as a colour which increases physiological arousal and it will also be described as 'exciting' and 'active', which rather suggests that it could induce movement or action of both mind and body. Red and the other fully saturated hues — particularly orange and yellow — appear to be ideal colours for incorporation into dynamic spaces where bodily locomotion, physical tasks or circulation are involved, such as corridors, stairways, entrance halls, bathrooms, toilets and, indeed, streets, concourses and pedestrian ways.

The authors have attempted to establish from their respective standpoints — art and psychology — that people enjoy and need more saturated colour in their external spaces. We need, therefore, to turn up the volume of environmental colour both through a much wider use of applied or intrinsic pigment in existing urban space and the integration of a more conscious approach into design programmes for future towns and cities. If we are to develop a more positive environmental colour approach we have to encourage more meaningful channels of information between the researcher and designer. If this book has come some way towards laying a foundation for a useful dialogue between environmental designer, the artist, and the psychologist, then we have achieved some success which, hopefully, might be reflected in a more colourful and therefore more psychologically rewarding future environment.

100
Rhesus monkey in testing chamber confronted by the back-projected image of a Vasarely painting.
Copyright *Sunday Times*.

144

Bibliography

Acking, C-A. & Küller, R.   'The Perception of an Interior as a Function of its Colour: (1) Colour of Interior Details' '(2) Colour of Interior Walls'. Lund Institute of Technology, Department of Theoretical and Applied Aesthetics, 1968 & 1969

Ardrey, R.   *The Territorial Imperative* Collins, London 1967

Bayes, K.   *The Therapeutic Effect of Environment on Emotionally Disturbed and Mentally Subnormal Children* Unwin, London 1967

Berlin, B. & Kay, P.   *Basic Colour Terms: Their Universality and Evolution* University of California Press, Berkeley 1969

Birren, F.   *Colour for Interiors* Whitney Library of Design, New York 1963

Birren, F.   'Colour and the Visual Environment' *Colour Engineering* July August 1971

Birren, F.   'Colour and Man-Made Environments' *The American Institute of Architects Journal* August 1972

Birren, F.   *Light, Colour and Environment* Van Nostrand Reinhold, New York 1969

Birren, F.   *Principles of Colour* Van Nostrand Reinhold, New York 1969

Blackemore, C.   'Development of the Brain Depends on the Visual Environment' *Nature* 228, London 1970

Burnham, R., Hanes, R., Bartleson,   *Colour: A Guide to Basic Facts and Concepts* John Wiley & Sons, New York 1963

Eysenck, H. J.   'A Critical and Experimental Study of Colour Preferences' *American Journal of Psychology* 54, 1941

Foss, M. *New Directions in Psychology* Penguin Books, Harmondsworth 1966

Goldstein, K. 'Some Experimental Observations Concerning the Influence of Colour on the Function of the Organism' *Occupational Therapy and Rehabilitation* Vol. 21, 1942

Goodman, S. H. 'Colour' Oxford Polytechnic, Department of Architecture 1973

Gregory, R. L. *Eye and Brain* Weidenfeld & Nicolson, London 1971

Hård, A. *The NCS Colour Order and Scaling System* Swedish Colour Centre, Stockholm 1969

Hogg, J. H. 'The Experience of Colour' *New Society* London, November 1970

Humphrey, N. K. 'Colour and Brightness Preferences in Monkeys' *Nature* 229, London 1970

Küller, R. *A Semantic Model for Describing Perceived Environment* National Swedish Institute for Building Research D12, Stockholm 1972

Küller, R. *Architectural Psychology,* proceedings of the Lund Conference 1973, Studentlitteratur ab, Sweden; Dowden Hutchinson, Pennsylvania 1973

Küppers, H. *Colour: Origin System Uses* Van Nostrand Reinhold, New York 1973

Linksz, A. *An Essay on Colour Vision* Grune & Stratton, New York 1964

Lüscher, M. *The Luscher Colour Test* Jonathan Cape, London 1970

MacNichol, E. F. Jnr. 'Three-Pigment Colour Vision' *Scientific American* December 1963

Osgood, C., Suci & Tannerbaum, P. H. *The Measurement of Meaning* University of Illinois Press, Urbana 1957

Payne, C. Jnr. 'Colour as an Independent Variable in Perceptual Research' *Psychology Bulletin* No. 3, 1964

Porter, T. 'An Investigation into Colour Preferences' *Designer* September 1973

Sivik, L. 'Colour Meaning and Perceptual Colour Dimensions: A Study of Exterior Colours' *Göteborg Psychology Reports* No. 11, University of Göteborg 1974

Index

Page numbers in italics refer to illustrations

149